The Korean Go Association's

Learn to Play Go

Volume II: The Way of the Moving Horse

Janice Kim 3 dan

Jeong Soo-hyun 9 dan

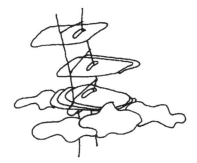

Drawings by **a lee**

Good Move Press

Published by
Good Move Press
PO Box 6984
Denver, CO 80206
www.samarkand.net

ISBN 0-9644796-2-1

Printed in Canada

CONTENTS

Preface and Acknowledgements

Volume II is the direct continuation of Volume 1. I recommend that you review Volume I before reading this one, but it's not strictly essential. Volumes II and III in the series are designed to take the reader to about 12 *gup* or *kyu*.

It was my intention to make it possible for those who only read Volume I to have all the information they need to play go. Concepts which were not introduced until this volume were briefly included in Volume I. In an effort to keep it simple, certain terms were used that are unwieldy or imprecise in more advanced books. The biggest change in terminology is the word *hane* for "turn the corner." The new terminology is introduced gradually to give readers a chance to familiarize them selves with new words.

The first three volumes are the introductory series, designed to give the reader the most solid foundation possible for quick progress. For that reason, stronger players who wish to wait for more advanced books are encouraged to review earlier volumes to make sure there are no gaps or "weak points" in your game. On the other hand, every effort is made to make the more advanced books accessible to new or inexperienced players, by avoiding jargon and analysis requiring specific prior knowledge, for example, "This high kakari in response to the nozoki is brilliant, showing a deep grasp of the fundamentals" becomes, "White 1, ignoring Black's threat, means to give up the smaller area on the right in order to take the bigger area on the left."

As always, I've tried to stick like a barnacle to Mr. Jeong's teaching, but any mistakes here are strictly my own. (I have also added some commentary, in which personal pronouns refer to me, and not to Mr. Jeong, unless clearly stated.) Many, many thanks to the reviewers of this book and Volume I, and also to Michael Simon, Philyoung Kim, Paul Agresti, Barbara London, David Mechner, Timothy Greenfield-Sanders, and Angie Lee for contributing their talented efforts to this project. Additional thanks go to the Hankook Kiwon, the Nihon Ki-in, my family and friends, and to my students, who teach me more than I teach them.

Janice Kim

June 21, 1995

Note to the 2nd Edition

Volume II of the Learn to Play Go series represents what I think may be a new way of looking at go for English speakers, based on what I call the "strength vs. speed" model I learned at the Korean Go Academy. While this book is designed for those who have read Volume I, and to be accessible to double-digit "gup" or "kyu" players generally, I hope it offers a fresh go perspective even for very experienced players, or those who are interested in the theory and philosophy of go and strategy games. The internal debates and breakfast meeting discussions I've had about such subjects as translating a Korean word into "extending" or "stretching" have proven unexpectedly rich for me – I would be very pleased if readers experience the charm of thinking about these kinds of things (not to mention the additional bonus that this may be of soon-to-be-discovered cosmic significance).

As with the second editions of Volumes I and III, this second edition of Volume II is only slightly different from the first. The main changes are that I've been striving for more clarity, and the layout has been changed to make it a bit easier to read, and I've gotten a chance to correct my mistakes, which makes me inordinately pleased (I've found that no one seems to take me seriously when I suggest putting tiny little stickers over typos in each book – now I get a whole new printing, so they don't drive me crazy.) I've also made some modifications based on helpful comments by readers of the first edition, particularly in my adoption of the convention of using "he" for Black and "she" for White, and a reworking of the Synthesis chapter, suggested by Brian D'Amato.

Additional thanks go to Michael Samuel, who created the new cover; one-man support group Bruce Price; Liz Shura and Team Samarkand; friends and family members, including the D'Amatos and Lottie; and to the readers of the first edition of this book and the other volumes in the Learn to Play Go series, who have been unceasingly supportive, kind, and generous with their time and efforts.

Janice Kim

October 21, 1998

Part 1:

PRINCIPLES

The ancient Egyptians learned the ideal way to build a pyramid through trial and error; collapsed structures built in different ways attest to this. In the same way, you could learn the basic principles of go by trial and error, but it's much easier just to read this book.

THE PROCESS OF GO

Go is a fight for territory. The player who has more territory wins, so each side concentrates on getting more than the other. Territory is made by surrounding empty areas on the board, but the best way to do this is not obvious. Those who are said to have a "knack for go" have learned principles and techniques for making territory.

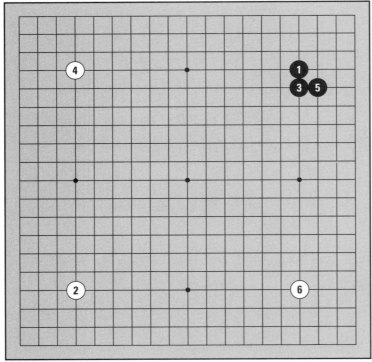

Diagram 1

Diagram 1:

Have a look at this opening. Black establishes a position in the upper right corner with 1, and White takes the lower left corner with 2. Next, Black plays at 3, right next to Black 1. White lays claim to another empty corner with 4. Black continues to surround the upper right corner with 5, and White takes the lower right corner with 6.

Diagram 2:

Black continues to block off the upper right corner with 7, 9, and 11. Finally, he completes a territory of twelve points with Black 15. In the meantime, White takes strategically important points from White 8 to White 16. Even though she doesn't have secure territory, White has taken almost all the important strategic points. In this diagram, which side is better?

You can answer this question by asking who stands to make more territory. Black made twelve points, but has stones in only one corner. White took many good points, so she has the beginnings of territory in many areas. White is better. This is an example of the first principle of making territory: playing stones right next to each other is a losing strategy, since each move only increases your territory by a small amount. So what is a better way?

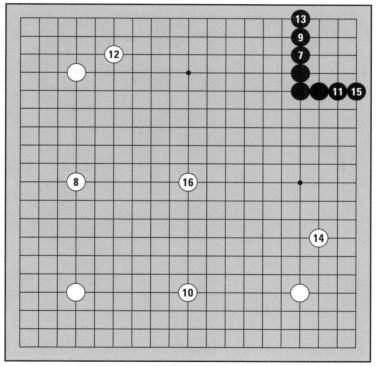

Diagram 2

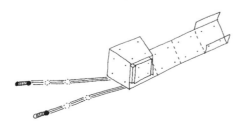

Diagram 3:

First, take important strategic points. This means staking a claim in the corners and sides, on or around the **star points** (one of the nine darker points on the board, used to locate your position).

Once you've staked a claim, you'll want to solidify these areas, by fighting if necessary. After the main fighting is over, each player then has to establish the borderlines of his or her territory. Most go games progress through these three stages, called the **opening, middle game,** and **endgame.**

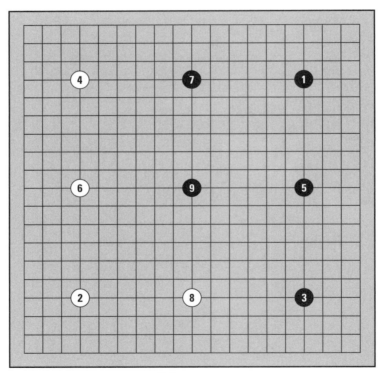

Diagram 3

1. The Opening

Taking important strategic points, outlining areas of potential territory, is called the **opening.**

Diagram 4:

Here both sides have taken important points from Black 1 to White 14. Even though not many stones have been played, doesn't it look like a lot of territory has been sketched out? Both sides have played the opening well, efficiently mapping out the basic shapes of their territory. Taking important strategic positions by putting your stones somewhat sparsely in big areas is the first step.

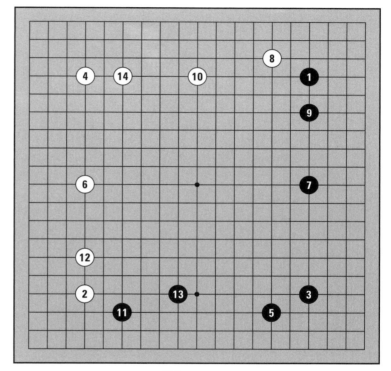

Diagram 4

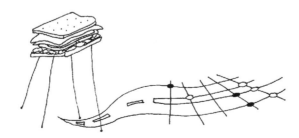

2. The Middle Game

The **middle game,** right after the opening, is the stage where real fighting starts. Even though go is about surrounding territory, it's often not so straightforward as just blocking it off. For example, your opponent may try to prevent you from making territory.

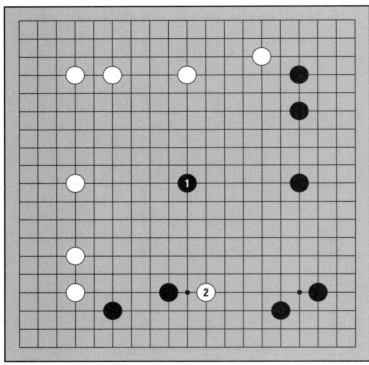

Diagram 5

Diagram 5:

When Black plays in the center with 1, White jumps into Black's area in the lower right with 2. White 2 means to break up this potential territory. Black's area is big, so instead of just giving it away, White feels compelled to fight for it.

Diagram 6:

Black 3 attacks. White is concerned that there isn't enough room to **live** (that is, make two separate points of territory) inside Black's area, so she jumps out with 4. Black pursues with 5 and White jumps again with 6. The chase continues from Black 7 to Black 11.

In the middle game, fighting is often about chasing and being chased. Territory is solidified through this kind of fighting.

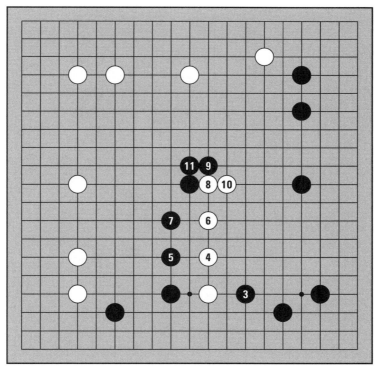

Diagram 6

Diagram 7:

The white group surrounds some space around A with 12 to 18. White has room to make two **eyes** (two separate points for living) now, so she has survived the attack. But while White was trying to make enough space to live, Black solidified territory on the right side with 13, 15, and 17. In the process of attacking White's invasion, Black has almost completed a large territory along the right side.

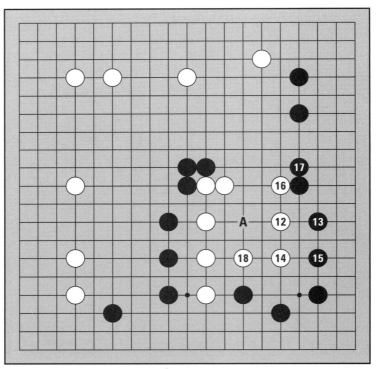

Diagram 7

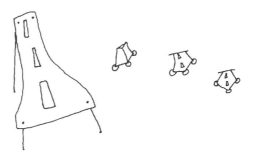

3. The Endgame

After the middle game, each side's territory is nearly determined, but the borderlines are still incomplete. The stage of go where the borderlines are completed is called the **endgame.**

Diagram 8:

Both sides have sectioned off some territory. Black's territory is on the right side, and White has some territory on top, but the borderlines aren't completely finished. For example, the border around A hasn't been determined yet.

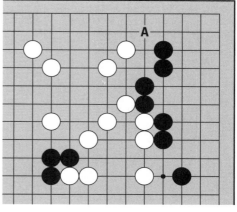

Diagram 8

Diagram 9:

If it is Black's turn, he can play at 1. White needs to block at 2 to keep the territory on the top. Black "turns the corner" (plays *hane*, in Gospeak) at 3 and White blocks at 4. Next, Black connects at 5, and White connects at 6.

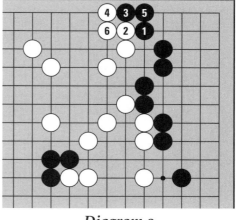

Diagram 9

An effective strategy is to follow the three stages of go—the opening, middle game, and endgame. First, take important points. Second, solidify your territory and contest your opponent's territory by fighting. Finally, complete the borderlines.

2

THE KNACK OF THE OPENING

In the opening, players sketch out territorial bases by putting stones in key positions. A good opening, like a good foundation, will enable you to build large structures. There is a knack to the opening, which you can develop by following certain basic principles.

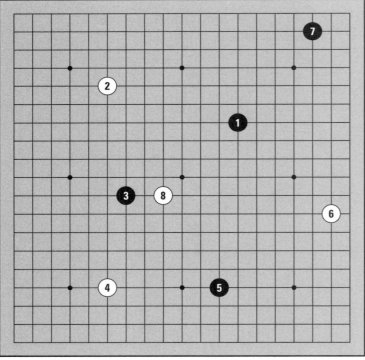

Diagram 1

Diagram 1:

Here stones are scattered in a disorderly fashion. This kind of random play is not good opening strategy. Compare this with the next diagram.

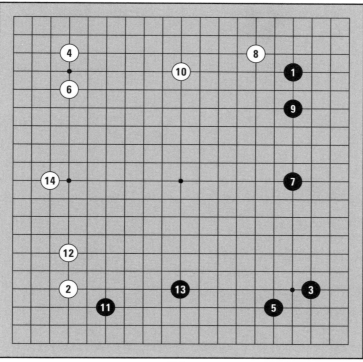

Diagram 2

Diagram 2:

This is a normal opening. What's the difference? Stones placed in an orderly fashion follow these principles:

1. **Start from the corners.**

2. **After the corners, go to the sides.**

3. **Use the third and the fourth lines.**

These are the three basic rules of the opening.

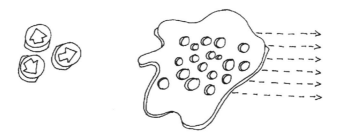

1. *Start from the corners.*

Diagram 3:

What's the reason for starting in the corners? Take a look at the diagram below. Black has made nine points in each area: in the center, on the side, and in the corner. But each time he used a different number of stones to take the same nine points—six stones in the corner, nine for the side, and twelve in the center. From this you can deduce that the corner is the most efficient place to make territory. After the corners, go to the sides. The center is the least efficient area for making territory, so during the opening put stones in the center last.

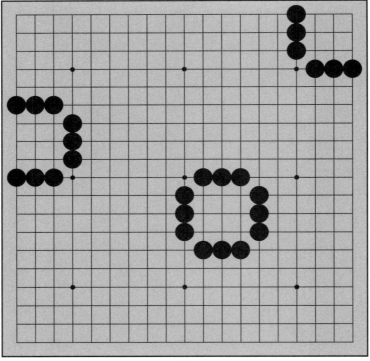

Diagram 3

Now you know to start from the corners, but where in the corner should you put your stones?

Diagram 4:

There are five or six standard ways to take empty corners. The star point at 1 and the move at 2 are played most often. White 2 is called the **3-4 point**.

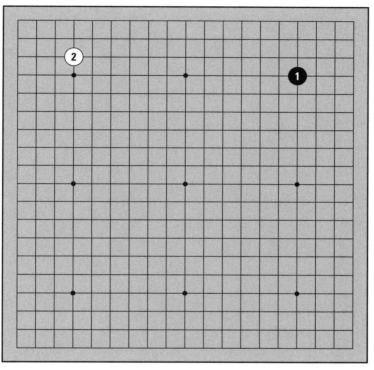

Diagram 4

We call it the 3-4 point because it is three lines from one edge and four lines from another. Other points named this way are the **3-3 point**, the **5-4 point**, and the **5-3 point** (which number goes first is just a matter of convention).

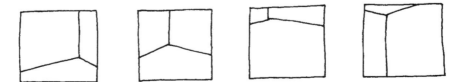

2. *After the corners, go to the sides.*

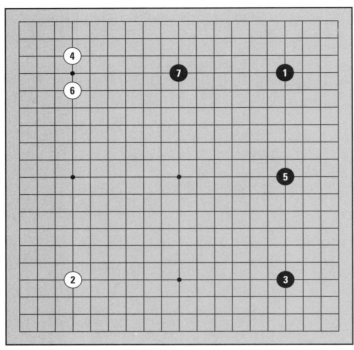

Diagram 5

Diagram 5:

Here's an opening that was played by Lee Chang-ho (then 4 dan) and Jeong Soo-hyun (then 6 dan). After Lee took empty corners with Black 1 and 3, he played on the right side with 5. When Jeong defended the upper left corner with 6, Lee played on the upper side with 7. Black 5 and 7 are big opening points. Whoever takes the big points first stands to make a lot of profit.

••• Go Statistics •••••••••••••••••

According to a recent survey, 18% of the Korean population plays go. An estimated 10% of the population of Japan and China also play, so the number of go players world-wide probably exceeds 100 million. Just as nearly all Westerners recognize the game of chess and some chess terminology, nearly all Asians recognize go and know some go terminology, even if they do not actually play. Major newspapers and television networks in Asia sponsor tournaments which are widely followed, and there are entire magazines, newspapers, and a TV network devoted solely to go coverage. One of the most widely viewed films of all time is *The Go Masters,* and two Nobel prizewinning authors, Kawabata and Hesse, have written novels using go as a backdrop. Go predates all other games currently played by at least a thousand years, and the number of possible combinations of moves is said to exceed the number of subatomic particles in the universe. Small wonder go is often called the ultimate game.

3. *Use the third and fourth lines.*

"Third" or "fourth" line means the third or fourth line from the edge of the board.

Diagram 6:

Black puts a stone on the upper side at 1. Black 1 is on the third line from the edge.

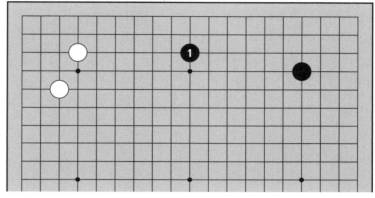

Diagram 6

Diagram 7:

Black 1 here is on the fourth line. In both Diagram 6 and here, Black 1 is a well-placed move.

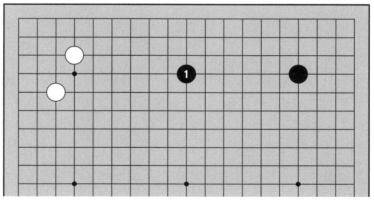

Diagram 7

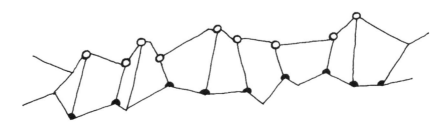

Diagram 8:

Putting a stone on the second line is too close to the edge. This will be ineffective for making territory, because White 2 easily prevents Black from claiming a large area.

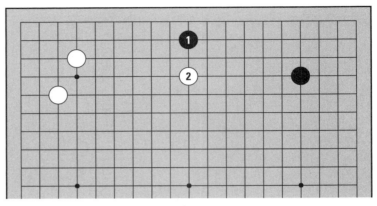

Diagram 8

Diagram 9:

Black 1 on the fifth line is too far from the edge. If White puts a stone at 2, Black has difficulty making territory on the upper side. Black 1 is best on the third or fourth line.

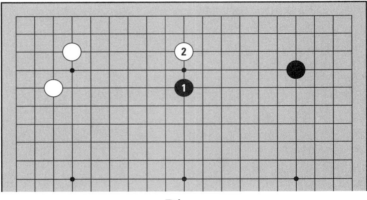

Diagram 9

Cho Chi-hoon 9 dan (left) takes on an unidentified member of the new generation of Go players, while a time keeper and game recorder look on.

photo: Nihon Kiin

Yoda Norimoto 9 dan, one of the leading players of the young generation in Japan.

Michael Redmond 8 dan, a native of California, plays a game on Japanese television.

photo: Nihon Kiin

3

Enclosures and Approaches

After the corners, go to the sides. What's next after the sides? Reinforcing your corners, or approaching your opponent's corners, is a good strategy. If a corner isn't reinforced, an approach may obstruct it from becoming territory.

1. The Enclosure

The enclosure is a defensive move to secure corner territory.

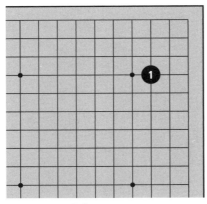

Diagram 1

Diagram 1:

Black takes an empty corner at 1, but playing just this one stone doesn't make the corner his territory yet.

Diagram 2:

Black encloses the corner by playing at 2. This corner has become Black's territory.

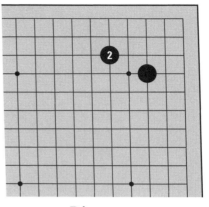

Diagram 2

Diagram 3:

Even though Black has played only two stones, the corner already has a hidden border-line along the points marked X.

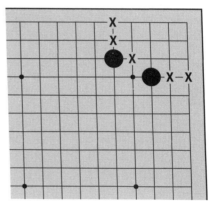

Diagram 3

Diagram 4:

If White plays at 1 with the intention of breaking through his enclosure, Black can block at 2 with no problem (if White tries to cut at A, Black can, for example, just capture the cutting stone by driving it to the edge with B).

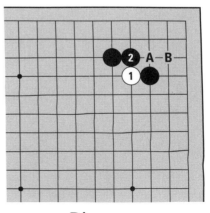

Diagram 4

Diagram 5:

When the first move is on a 3-4 point, the two main ways to enclose a corner are at Black 1 and White 2. Black's enclosure is called the **knight's enclosure,** and White's is called the **one-point enclosure.**

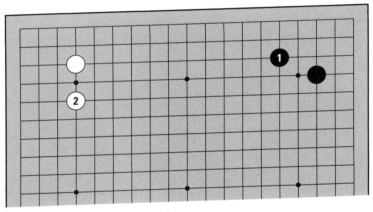

Diagram 5

Diagram 6:

From the star points, one can also make a knight's enclosure. The difference is that Black needs an additional stone at A to secure the corner territory.

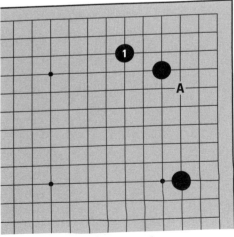

Diagram 6

Diagram 7:

Black 1 here is a one-point enclosure starting from the star point. Again, you'll need one more enclosing stone to secure territory in the corner.

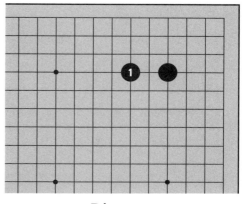

Diagram 7

Diagram 8:

White can make territory in the upper left corner with just one move, but Black has to play twice to secure the upper right corner territory.

3-4 point corner territory: 1 more move

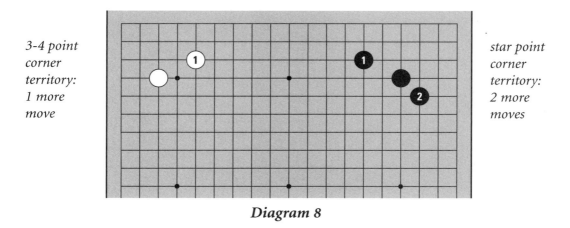

star point corner territory: 2 more moves

Diagram 8

Opening Tip: it's more efficient to make territory from a 3-4 point than from a star point, because it takes one less move. That's why we commonly rush to enclose the corner from a 3-4 point, but adopt a leisurely attitude about enclosing the corner from the star point. Note this is not to say that you shouldn't play the star point. It's just that you should think about enclosing 3-4 point corners, approaching your opponent's corners, or playing one of the big points on the side before rushing to enclose a star point corner.

2. *The Approach*

If you don't make an enclosure, your opponent can make an approach.

Diagram 9:

White 1 approaches the black stone on the upper right star point. This obstructs Black's potential enclosure of the corner. This is called the **knight's approach,** because White 1 has a **knight's move** relationship with the Black star point stone.

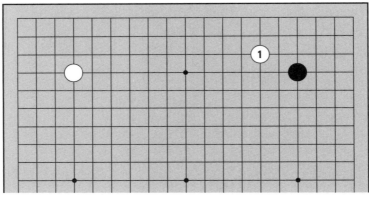

Diagram 9

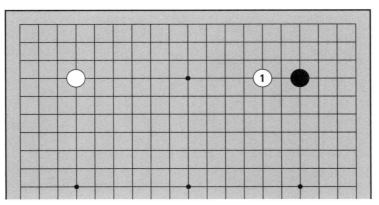

Diagram 10

Diagram 10:

White 1 here is another approach move. This is called the **one-point approach,** because White 1 is one point away from the Black star point stone.

Diagram 11:

How about a closer approach like White 1? This move, making direct contact with the black stone, is called an **attachment.** The attachment here is an attempt to provoke a direct fight.

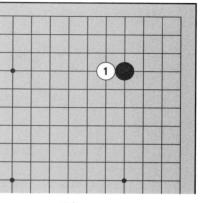

Diagram 11

Diagram 12:

Black has a strong counterattack. In this fight White is outnumbered, so the white stone is in danger.

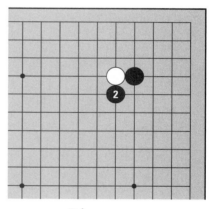

Diagram 12

Diagram 13:

If White runs at 3, Black connects at 4, gaining the superior position. (If White cuts at 4 instead, it's Black's turn in an even fight, so he should still come out better.) The attachment at 1 in *Diagram 11* doesn't usually work well in the opening, so this isn't a good approach move.

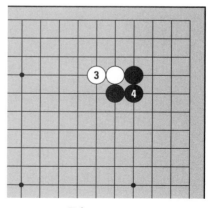

Diagram 13

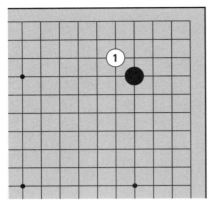

Diagram 14

Diagram 14:

How about White 1, a "diagonal approach"? This stone also approaches too closely.

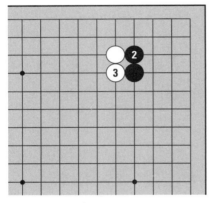

Diagram 15

Diagram 15:

Black blocks at 2. Then if White plays at 3—

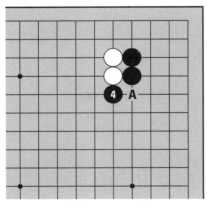

Diagram 16

Diagram 16:

Next Black hits White on the head with 4. Black 4 is called "hitting the head of two stones", an ideal position for the hitter, and painful for the hittee. (Once again, if White cuts at A, it's Black's turn in an even fight, so he should come out ahead.)

When you want to play near your opponent's corner, use the knight's or the one-point approach. They are both good.

The Hankook Kiwon

The Hankook Kiwon, or Korean Baduk (Go) Association, is the headquarters of Korean go. It was located for the past twenty years or so in Chongro-gu but recently moved to a new building in Wangshimri, both in Seoul. The new building is very elegant and retains the rooftop ping-pong table, but I miss the old building, where I attended the Korean Go Academy.

The members of the Hankook Kiwon are the slightly more than 100 Korean professional players. (This differs from the American Go Association, where players don't need any credentials besides an interest in go to become members.) A galaxy of dignified players such as Cho Hoon-hyun 9 dan, Cho Nam-chul 9 dan, and Kim In 9 dan take part in formal title matches in the Traditional Playing Room or the Tournament Room, while students play, review, and get into squid-throwing fights in the Student Hall.

The Hankook Kiwon also manages big amateur tournaments such as the Amateur Top Ten, the Amateur Guksoo, and the elementary, middle, high, and university-level championships. The Hankook Kiwon has a chairman (Kim Woo-chung, also chairman of Daewoo Corporation), a president, director general, board of directors, general affairs department, editorial staff, and publishing department. The material in this book was originally published in Korean by the Hankook Kiwon's publishing department.

4

ANSWERING THE APPROACH

An approach move is played close enough to the corner to be a threat, so one feels inclined to answer it. If you don't answer an approach move, you can be attacked.

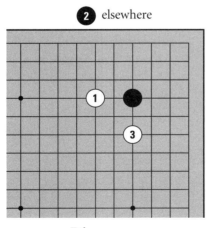

Diagram 1

Diagram 1:

White approaches the star point stone in the upper right corner at 1. If Black doesn't answer but plays 2 elsewhere, White can approach on the other side at 3. Now this black stone has become weak, hemmed in on both sides. Answering White 1 is a good idea.

1. Answering the Knight's Approach

Diagram 2:

White 1, a knight's approach to the star point stone, is one of the most popular moves. How should Black answer?

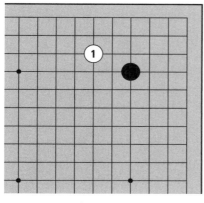

Diagram 2

Diagram 3:

There are many ways to answer, but the jump at 2 is one of the most common. Black 2 means to protect against White's approach on the other side.

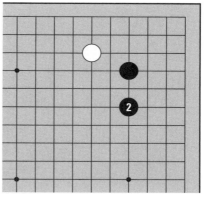

Diagram 3

Diagram 4:

If White plays at 3, Black can answer at 4.

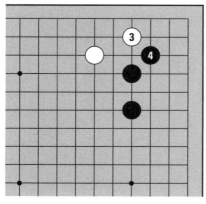

Diagram 4

Diagram 5:

Often White jumps to 5, and Black makes an extension along the side with 6. This is a very common sequence.

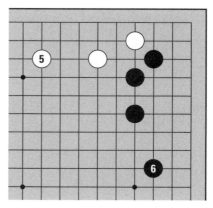

Diagram 5

Diagram 6:

This is a game between two professional players. When White plays the knight's approach to the star point stone with 1, Black jumps at 2. Then when White slides into the corner with 3, Black answers at 4. Finally White makes a base at 5 and Black takes a big point at 6. White's shape is very good, so many people play this sequence as a continuation to the knight's approach. This type of popular sequence, that makes good shape and good sense for both sides, is called *joseki* in Japanese and *jeongsuk* in Korean. In Volume I, we called this a "standard sequence."

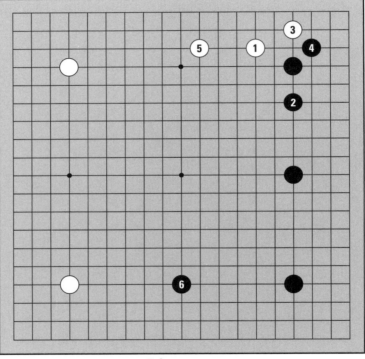

Diagram 6

Since I can't say the word *joseki* without remembering an excruciatingly embarrassing experience at the Korean Go Academy, I'll use the term **pattern.**

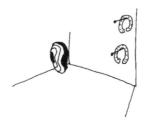

2. Answering the One-Point Approach

Diagram 7:

When White plays the one point approach to the star point stone, how should Black answer?

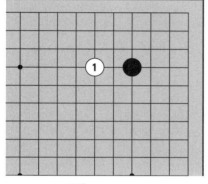

Diagram 7

Diagram 8:

The jump here is a good answer. Black 2 protects his interests in the corner.

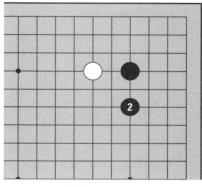

Diagram 8

Diagram 9:

If White continues with the attachment at 3, Black can turn the corner (that is, play *hane*), blocking White with 4.

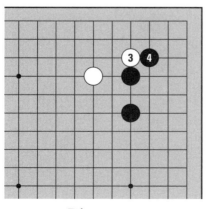

Diagram 9

Diagram 10:

White needs to connect these stones by pulling back at 5. Now Black can take the corner territory by coming straight down to the edge with 6. White once again needs to make a base with 7, and Black makes a large territory with 8. This is another pattern which is useful to know.

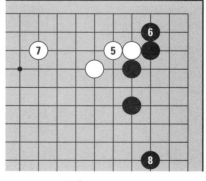

Diagram 10

5

BASES AND EXTENSIONS

*You should always consider the stability of your stones. This means that your stones have to have a **base,** or a territory in which you can make at least two eyes. Stones without a base can be killed, so making bases is very important.*

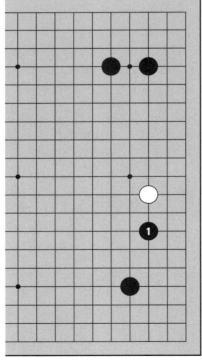

Diagram 1

Diagram 1:

Black approaches at 1. How should White play?

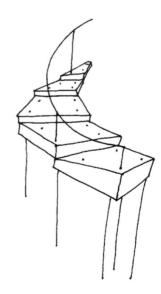

Diagram 2:

If White doesn't defend, Black can attack with 3 and White won't have a base. Stones without a base are weak, so it is not good for White to ignore Black 1.

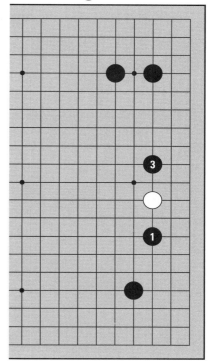

② elsewhere

Diagram 2

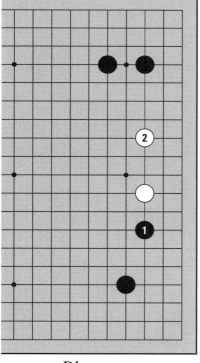

Diagram 3

Diagram 3:

Making a base by playing at 2 is a good idea. Moves like White 2, sketching out territory on the side, are called **extensions.**

1. *"If one, jump two; if two, jump three"*

There is a saying about extensions: "if one, jump two; if two, jump three." This means jumping two points from one stone and three points from two stones.

Diagram 4:

Black approaches at 1. What if White plays the extension at 2? This is a wild move. The extension here is too wide.

Diagram 5:

White's stones are too far apart, so Black can easily separate them with 3.

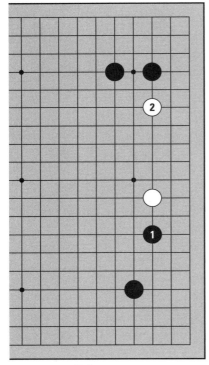

Diagram 4

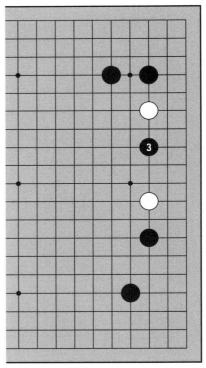

Diagram 5

Diagram 6:

How about playing at 1? This is too narrow. If Black approaches at 2, White can't make a large enough base to live.

Diagram 7:

White 1, the **two-point extension**, is correct. This makes a large enough base, but the stones can't be readily split apart.

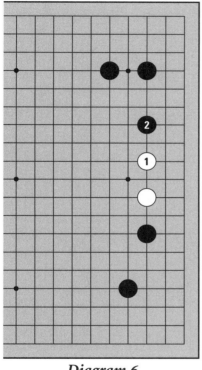

Diagram 6

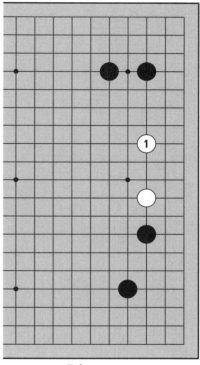

Diagram 7

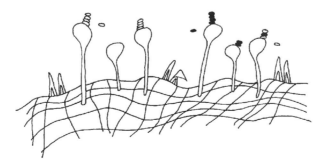

Diagram 8:

If Black tries to cut the two-point extension, what will happen? White can play at either A or 2, but White 2 is better.

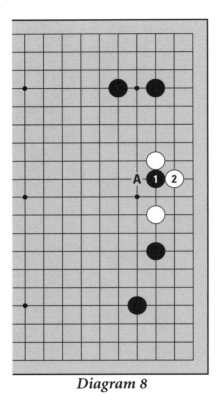

Diagram 8

Diagram 9:

If Black tries to cut with 3, White can cut at 4, so one black stone is in **atari**.* Next if Black runs at 5, White connects at 6. If Black plays A in an attempt to save Black 3, White can trap Black at B, so White can't be cut.

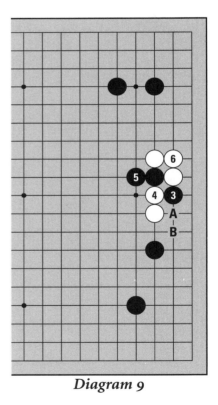

Diagram 9

* An atari is a move which threatens to capture on the next move, i.e. reducing remaining liberties to one.

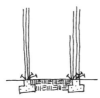

Diagram 10:

Black played the knight's approach to the star point stone. If White plays at 1, Black goes straight up with 2, and White jumps at 3.

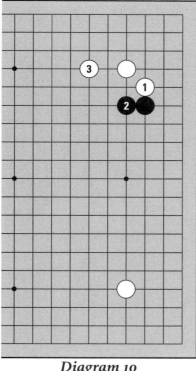

Diagram 10

Diagram 11:

Next, if Black doesn't play around here, White can attack at 1, which interferes with Black's base. Black has difficulty living with these stones.

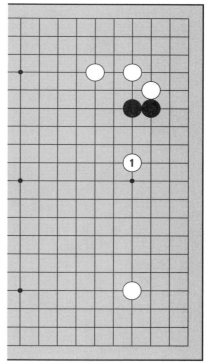

Diagram 11

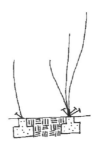

Diagram 12:

It is important for Black to make a base. Black 1 is a **three-point extension.** When two black stones are standing in a row, a three-point extension is the standard move.

Diagram 13:

Black 1, a two-point extension, is a little narrow.

Diagram 14:

If White tries to cut the three-point extension at 1, Black can connect underneath with 2 and 4.

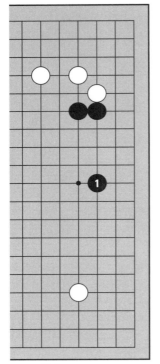

Diagram 12

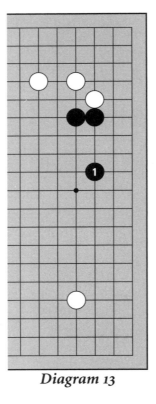

Diagram 13

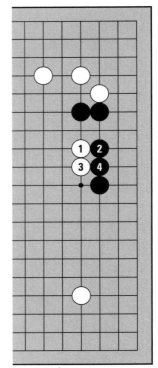

Diagram 14

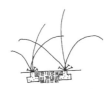

Diagram 15:

If White attacks at 1 here, Black can play on top with 2. Black 4 is beginning to enclose the "attacking" stones. White's situation has become perilous.

Diagram 16:

If White plays at 3 here, Black can cut at 4. Again, White's outnumbered "attacking" stones are in trouble.

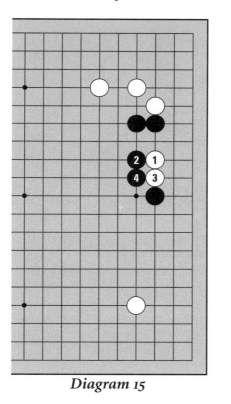

Diagram 15

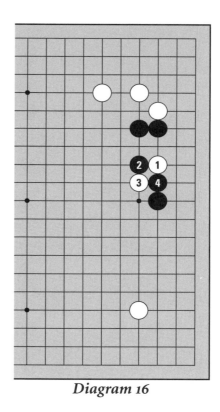

Diagram 16

What It Means: With one stone, a two-point jump is a good extension. From two stones, a three-point jump is a good extension. In each case, the extension makes the largest possible base, while remaining connected.

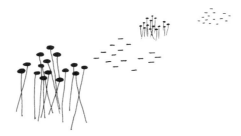

THE WAY OF THE MOVING HORSE

The way stones "run" or "move" is called **haengma**. A group of stones is called ma or "horse" in Korean, so haengma is something like the Way of the Moving Horse.

Stones can't move after they are played, but you can connect your stones together to form chains or groups. As the game progresses and more stones are added, the chains of stones look like they are "running" or "moving" across the board. Or so it seemed to ancient go players; you may prefer to think of haengma as simply the relationship between two of your stones.

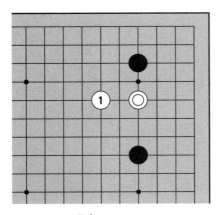

Diagram 1

Diagram 1:

White jumps out at 1. Her intention is to move White ⊚ out of danger.

Diagram 2:

Next Black played at 2 in order to develop the side. White jumped out again at 3, and Black continued with 4. White's and Black's moves here have a relationship with pre-existing stones—in this case, they are all **one-point jumps.** A one-point jump is an example of *haengma*, "the way the horse moves". There are six basic *haengma*. Choosing which *haengma* to use is a matter of balancing strength and speed, and deciding which direction you want your horse to go.

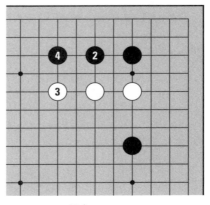

Diagram 2

1. *Stretching*

Diagram 3:

Black 1, played right on an adjacent liberty, is called **stretching** (this was previously called "extending", but since this may be confused with a "side extension", you may want to use the new term). This move is very strong, but slow.

Diagram 4:

One often stretches toward the edge to defend territory. It's not the most efficient move for surrounding territory, but it is very secure.

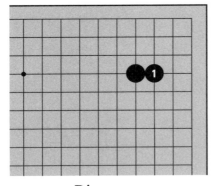

Diagram 3

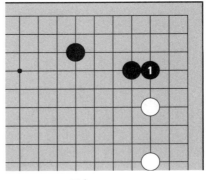

Diagram 4

2. *The One-Point Jump*

Diagram 5:

As you've seen, Black 1, skipping over one point, is called the one-point jump. This move is also strong (it retains connectivity) but a little faster (it travels one point farther) than stretching.

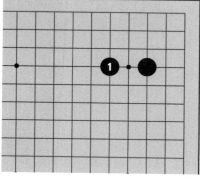

Diagram 5

Diagram 6:

The one-point jump is commonly used for escape. Here, if Black approaches at 1, White can escape with a one-point jump at 2. If Black plays at 3, White can play another one-point jump at 4.

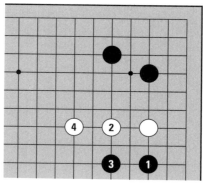

Diagram 6

3. *The Two-Point Jump*

Diagram 7:

Black 1 is the **two-point jump.** It is faster than one-point jump, but not as strong. It is often used as a side extension.

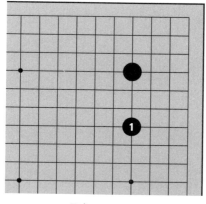

Diagram 7

4. *The Diagonal*

Diagram 8:

White 1, as you may have seen in Volume I, is called the **diagonal.** The diagonal is a type of connection, so it is very strong, but a bit slow.

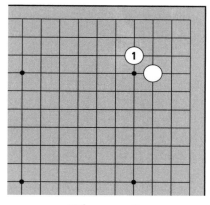

Diagram 8

Diagram 9:

If Black approaches at ⬤, White can play the diagonal at 1. This strengthens White's position and puts pressure on Black ⬤.

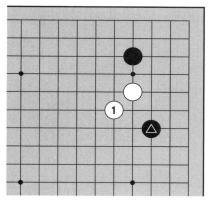

Diagram 9

5. *The Knight's Move*

Diagram 10:

Black 1, in relation to ⬤, is called the **knight's move.** This haengma is strong and fast, so it is often used in attacking, driving opposing stones in the desired direction.

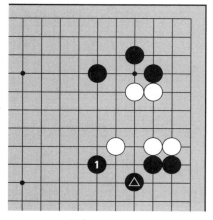

Diagram 10

Diagram 11:

The knight's move is also used to surround territory. Here, Black can attack at A, separating the white stones. How can White defend?

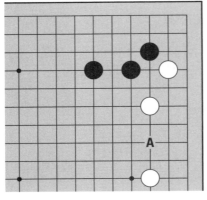

Diagram 11

Diagram 12:

The knight's move is particularly good in this case, completely surrounding the territory on the upper right side.

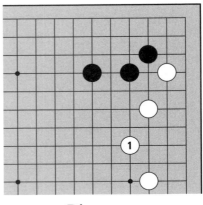

Diagram 12

6. The Large Knight's Move

Diagram 13:

White 1 is the **large knight's move.** It's a bit loose, but very fast.

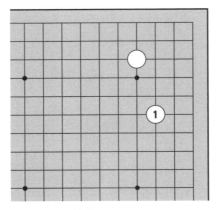

Diagram 13

Diagram 14:

Black 1 here is not a particularly strong move, but it does surround territory quickly.

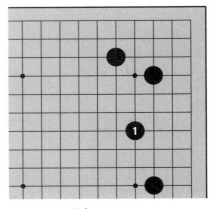

Diagram 14

7. *Weak Haengma*

Diagram 15:

Black 1, a "double diagonal," is called the **field.**

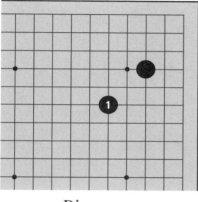

Diagram 15

Diagram 16:

If White plays right in the middle at 2, Black can't connect.

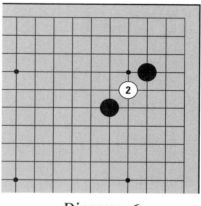

Diagram 16

Diagram 17:

If Black plays at 3, White slices through the knight's move at 4. The field is easily cut, so it is very weak and not recommended.

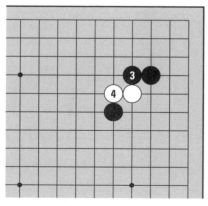

Diagram 17

Diagram 18:

Black 1 is also poorly related—White can easily cut these stones by playing at A or B. Try to avoid moves like Black 1, the "crippled horse".

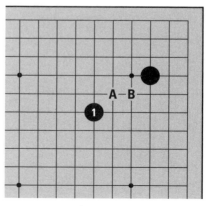

Diagram 18

7

INVASION AND REDUCTION

The middle game is the stage of fighting and making territory. Areas that have been loosely claimed in the opening are often contested.

1. *Invasion*

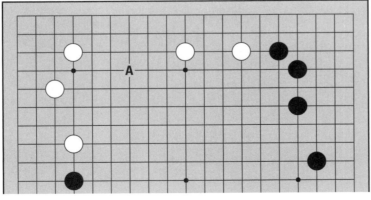

Diagram 1

Diagram 1:

White's stones on the upper side are far apart. If White plays at A, she will control this area. If it is Black's turn, where can he play to prevent this?

Diagram 2:

Black can jump in at 1. This is called an **invasion** of White's area on the upper side.

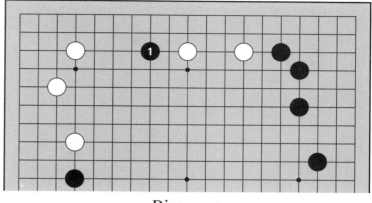

Diagram 2

Diagram 3:

If White plays at 2, Black can escape with the one-point jump at 3. Next if White continues the attack with 4, Black can jump again with 5. Black has broken up White's area, so his invasion has succeeded.

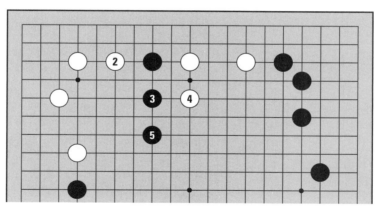

Diagram 3

Diagram 4:

When Black invades at 1, White can attempt to surround him with 2. In this case Black can't escape easily, so he has to live in White's area.

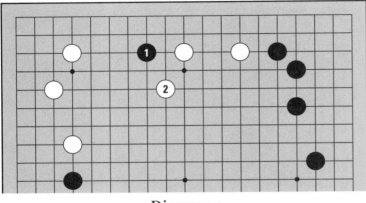

Diagram 4

Diagram 5:

First, Black can play at 3. If White blocks with 4 and 6, next Black can make a base with 7. He has to make two separate points of territory in order to live, so—

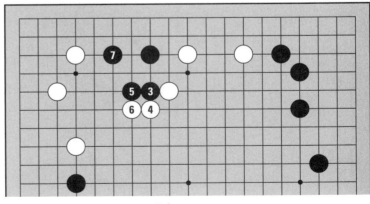

Diagram 5

Diagram 6:

If White continues to surround him with 8 and 10, Black plays at 11. Black 11 is a vital point for making two eyes. Black lives.

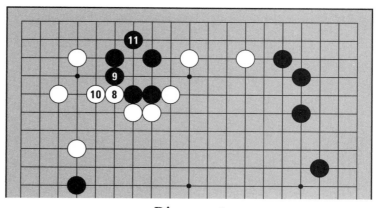

Diagram 6

Diagram 7:

If White plays at 1, Black 2 makes one eye. Next if White blocks at 3, Black secures life with 4. He has at least two separate points of territory, one at A and one at B, so he is alive. Even though surrounded, Black lives, so once again the invasion is a success. If Black can't make two eyes, he can be captured and the invasion is a failure.

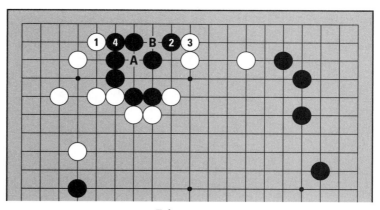

Diagram 7

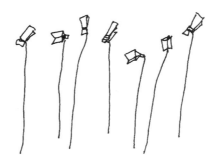

2. Reduction

A **reduction** is also a means to break up or reduce the opponent's territory, but a reduction isn't as deep as an invasion.

Diagram 8:

Black 1 here is possible too. Black 1 is a reduction of White's area on the upper side. This move seems to touch the shoulder of White's stone, so it is called the **shoulder hit.**

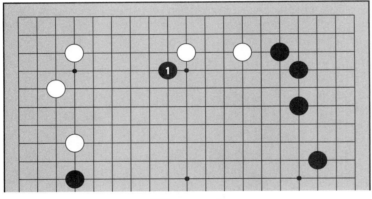

Diagram 8

Diagram 9:

If White plays 2, Black extends with 3. Black's two stones are out in the center, so he doesn't have to worry that these stones will be surrounded.

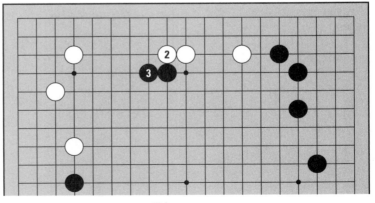

Diagram 9

Diagram 10:

If White continues at 4, Black continues to extend at 5. White can make territory on the upper side with 6 and 8, but this is not bad for Black. With 9 Black has made a strong wall facing the center. This kind of wall creates **influence** or **power.** Power is not territory, but it can be useful in future fighting. Black's reduction can also be judged a success, because even though White made some territory, she had stones here to begin with. Black has successfully prevented the expansion of White's area, and has made influence in the center.

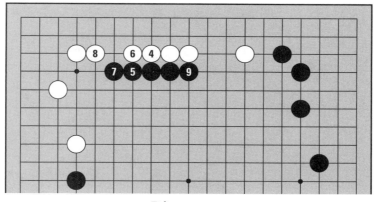

Diagram 10

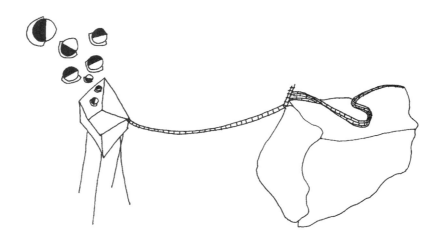

Diagram 11:

Where should White play to reduce Black's area?

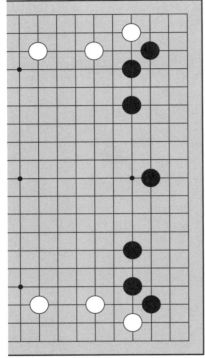

Diagram 11

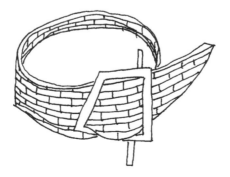

Diagram 12:

Black can play at 1 if White doesn't play here. This is a good point for defense, solidifying a lot of territory, so White would like to reduce here first.

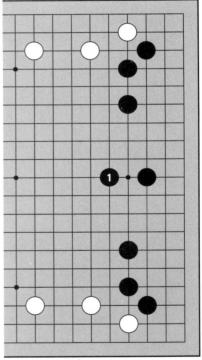

Diagram 12

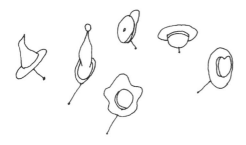

Diagram 13:

White 1 is a vital point for reduction. This is called a **capping move**, or just a **cap** – an enemy stone sitting on your head one point away. The idea is to reduce Black's area on the right side.

Diagram 14:

If Black plays at 2, White can play at 3. Next if Black extends at 4 and White makes a two-point jump into the center with 5, this result is pretty good for White. Again, Black has made some territory, but White has successfully reduced Black's area and has influence in the center.

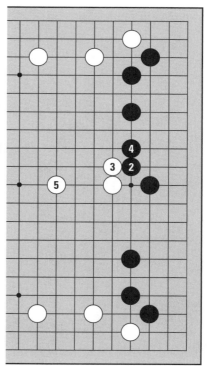

Diagram 14

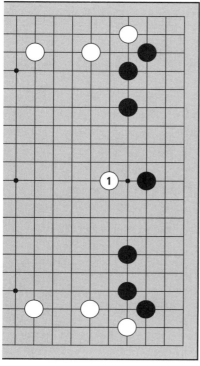

Diagram 13

Top Japanese player Kobayashi Koichi 9 dan strikes a typical pose.

Honda Sachiko 6 dan (left) and Aoki Kikuyo 6 dan compete for the Women's Honinbo title.

Photos: Nihon Kiin

Part II:

SKILLS

Among other things, the Go board is a battle-field, and a skillful Go player is one who is skilled in fighting.

8

How to Attack

To attack means to chase stones that are not alive yet.

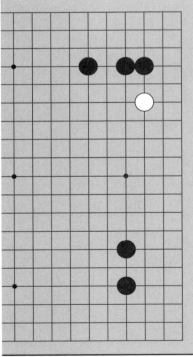

Diagram 1

Diagram 1:

The white stone on the upper right side is not alive yet. If it is Black's turn, White can be attacked.

Diagram 4:

White continues with 4, since if these stones are surrounded, they can be killed. This sequence is favorable for Black, because his area is expanding.

Diagram 3:

If White escapes by jumping to 2, Black can give chase with 3. Notice that while attacking, Black is also expanding his area on the right side.

Diagram 2:

The approach at Black 1 is a severe attack, preventing the white stone from making a base. White has to run.

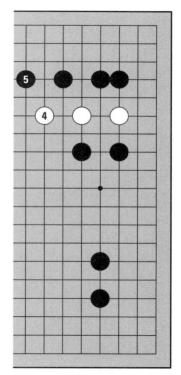

Diagram 4

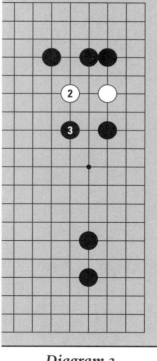

Diagram 3

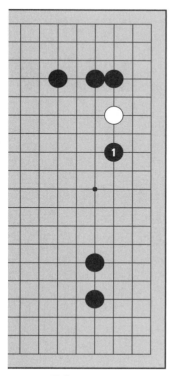

Diagram 2

1. How to Attack an Invading Stone

If you want to keep what is yours, you'll need to learn how to kill invaders.

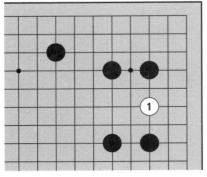

Diagram 5

Diagram 5:

A white invasion here is reckless. This stone can be attacked severely because Black's formation is very strong.

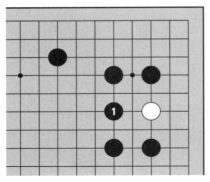

Diagram 6

Diagram 6:

Black 1 traps the stone.

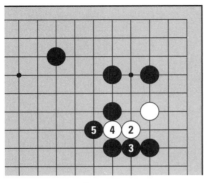

Diagram 7

Diagram 7:

If White tries to break out with 2, Black frustrates her plan with 3. Even if White continues with 4, these stones can't escape when Black blocks at 5.

Diagram 8:

If White tries to live by adding stones at 2 and 4, Black can just block at 3 and 5. White can make one eye by playing at A, but it is not enough to live. Since White can't escape, this group is dead. Black's attack was right on target.

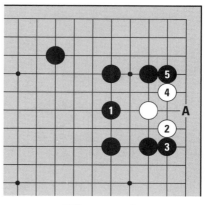

Diagram 8

Diagram 9:

The more enemy stones there are, the higher the odds of your being captured. Here, White plunges into Black's area at 1. Where should Black play to kill this stone?

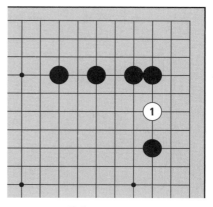

Diagram 9

Diagram 10:

Playing the capping move at Black 1 lets White escape through the field with 2.

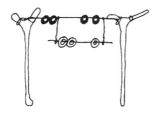

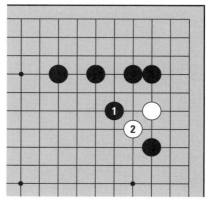

Diagram 10

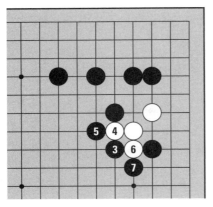

Diagram 11

Diagram 11:

The white stones appear to be surrounded by Black 3, but actually White can easily penetrate the enclosure with 4 and 6. Black 5 and 7 are not enough to prevent White from breaking through.

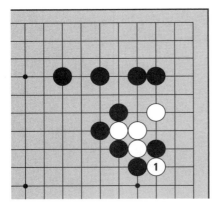

Diagram 12

Diagram 12:

If White cuts at 1, Black's wall can be broken because of its many defects.

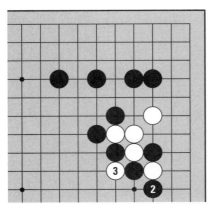

Diagram 13

Diagram 13:

After the cut and Black's atari at 2, White can play **double atari*** with 3.

* In double atari, two separate stones or groups are simultaneously threatened with capture.

Diagram 14:

If Black captures a stone at 4, White 5 captures a stone as well. Though both capture a stone, White has escaped, so Black's attack fizzles out. How can Black attack the invading stone more effectively?

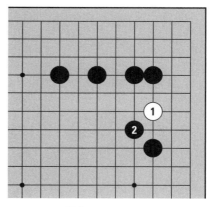

Diagram 14

Diagram 15:

The diagonal move at Black 2 is the best attack in this case. White is surrounded by this move.

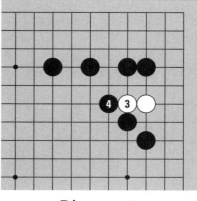

Diagram 15

Diagram 16:

If White tries to push up at 3, Black can block at 4. It's almost impossible for White to get out of here, thanks to the influence of the neighboring black stones.

Diagram 16

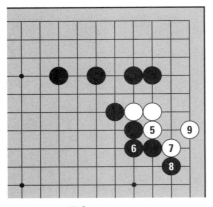

Diagram 17

Diagram 17:

If White tries to live at 5, Black can connect at 6, repairing the wall's defect. If White plays **hane** (turns the corner) at 7, Black blocks with 8. If White makes a **tiger's mouth** (three stones in a V-shape) at 9—

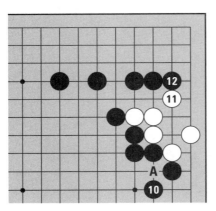

Diagram 18

Diagram 18:

The best offense is to remove the defect at A by making a tiger's mouth at 10. Finally, the white stones can't survive after the block at 12.

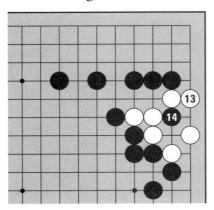

Diagram 19

Diagram 19:

Even if White tries to expand her eye space with 13, her group can be captured by a play at the vital center point with 14. Black has killed the invaders with a flawless attack.

Attacking and killing stones like this is a great success, since dead stones mean more territory for you and a reduction of your opponent's territory at the end of the game. However, it is not easy to kill invading stones.

Diagram 20:

White invades Black's extensive area at 1. Black's formation is too loose to kill the invading stone. In this case, what is the best move?

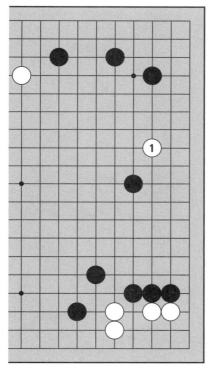

Diagram 20

Diagram 21:

How about trying to envelop White with 1? If White slips under the side star point stone at 2, she can make a base.

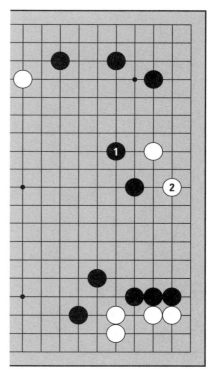

Diagram 21

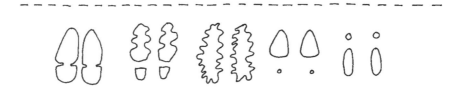

Diagram 22:

Black manages to prevent White from coming in further with 3, but if White pushes at 4 and Black responds at 5, then the extension at 6 gives her stones enough room to make two eyes, so they are alive.

Diagram 23:

Going back to the beginning, we can see that this formation is too loose to surround the invading stone. Instead, the **iron pillar** at Black 1 is a good move. Black 1 keeps White from making a base.

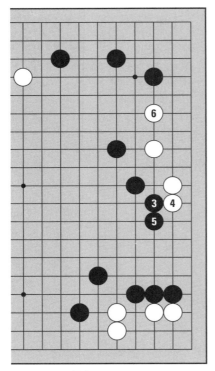

Diagram 22

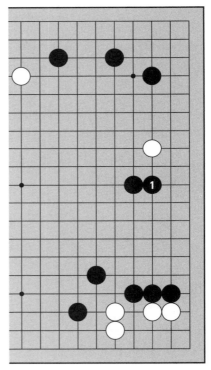

Diagram 23

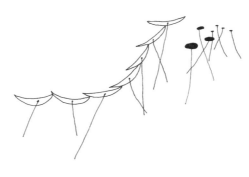

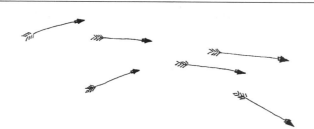

Diagram 24:

White doesn't have enough room to build a base now, so she runs at 2. Black can give chase with 3; if White 4, he continues with 5. Black can expand his territory on the lower right side by chasing the white group. An attack like this is effective even if you can't kill any stones.

Diagram 25:

After Black 1, if White plays somewhere else, then the cap at 2 is a severe attack. It's not easy for White to live inside after Black 1. If you have a loose formation, you shouldn't persist in trying to kill an invading stone. The best strategy is to expand your territory by chasing the invaders.

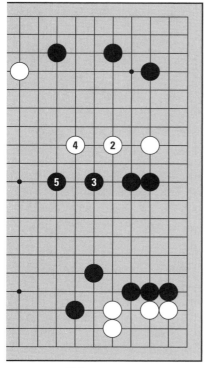

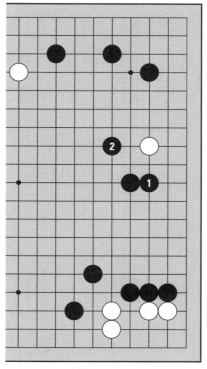

Diagram 24

Diagram 25

2. *When There are Weak Stones*

Diagram 26:

What is the best move to attack the white stone?

Diagram 27:

Black's approach at 1 is the most severe attack. Black 1, which works with Black ▲, is called a **pincer**.

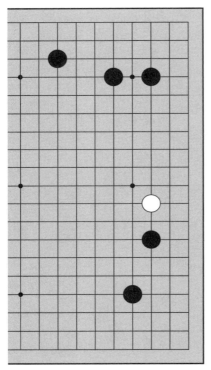

Diagram 26

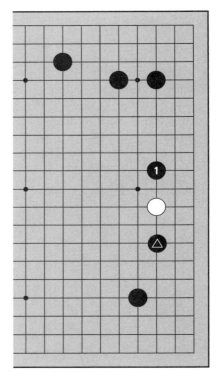

Diagram 27

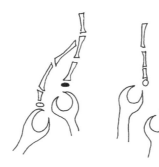

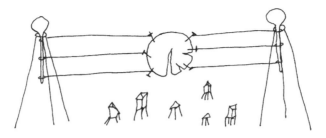

Diagram 28:

White can't get out of the vise. If White jumps, Black can give chase. In the wake of these maneuvers, Black claims an extensive area in the upper right. It's very good attacking technique to expand your area by chasing weak stones like this.

Diagram 29:

This situation often occurs in handicap games. White has two weak stones in the upper right corner. Black wants to attack them. What's a good attacking move?

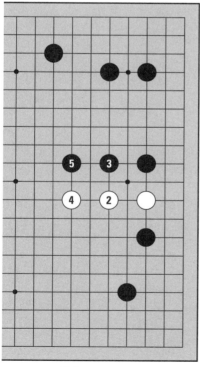

Diagram 28

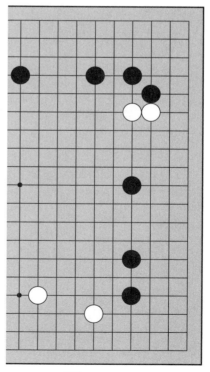

Diagram 29

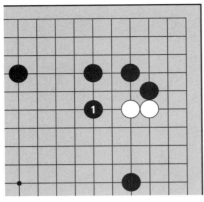

Diagram 30

Diagram 30:

Getting in the way with Black 1 is an effective attack.

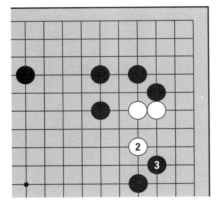

Diagram 31

Diagram 31:

If White dodges at 2, Black can play at 3. Black is expanding the area in the lower right and destroying White's base as well.

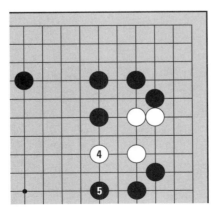

Diagram 32

Diagram 32:

White has to keep running with 4, so Black can continue the chase with 5. This sequence is favorable for Black.

Diagram 33:

Black 1 here is also a good attack, destroying White's base and expanding Black's area. Killing two birds with one stone like this is a very effective way of playing.

Diagram 34:

If White tries to get out with 2, Black can keep the pressure on with 3. This sequence is also favorable for Black.

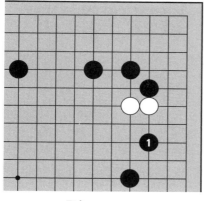

Diagram 33

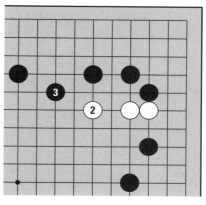

Diagram 34

As you have seen, an effective attack is a great way to take the initiative. I hope you'll be good at attacking; it's one of the most enjoyable things in go.

The Aim of Go

The aim of Go lies in taking more territory than your opponent. However, some people are more interested in capturing stones than in expanding their territories.

Once my teacher Jeong Soo-hyun taught a six-year-old how to play go. The boy liked to capture stones very much and was not interested in making territory. But capturing is not easy. If the boy embarked on a plan to capture some stones, they often escaped. The child appeared to get bored and angry when these attempts were fruitless. It was a difficult problem, because Teacher Jeong had sacrificed many of his stones at first to satisfy the boy's blood lust. Teacher Jeong had a hard time convincing this budding general not to be interested in capturing, but to be interested in making territory. As the general of your own armies, it is imperative that you keep the aim of go always in mind.

9

HOW TO DEFEND

Learning how to defend is as important as learning how to attack. There are two major types of defense: defense of territory, and defense of weak stones.

1. Defense of Territory

What is "territory?" There are many different Asian words for "territory," each with a slightly different connotation. This is because, I am told, Asians have a long and deep connection to their land, and thus make very fine distinctions which are difficult to translate. (Not a surprise that the most popular game in Asia would be about taking land, as opposed to taking prisoners as in chess.)

So far, we have been using the word "territory" in a strict sense, that is, an area which cannot be taken by force, but could be given in trade or lost by mistake. Some areas look like they are shaping up into territory, but may still have weak points in the walls or invasion points inside. Calling it "territory" before defending is optimistic. There are some techniques to learn to convert areas like this into territory (or "defend what is yours," if you are an optimist).

Diagram 1:

Take a look at the upper right corner. There is a defect in Black's wall. He has to be alert.

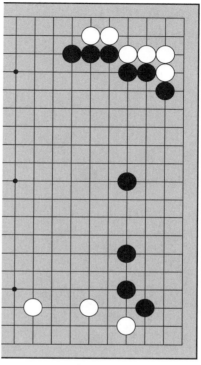

Diagram 1

Diagram 2:

This formation has a weak point that can be cut with White 1. Black's area can be destroyed easily with this move.

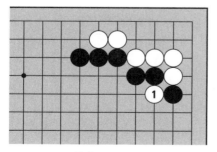

Diagram 2

Diagram 3:

If Black tries to drive White with 2 after the cut, White will run at 3. Black ▲, which was severed from the main force by the cut, is about to be captured.

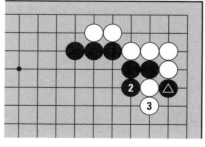

Diagram 3

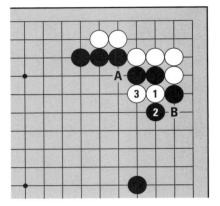

Diagram 4

Diagram 4:

If Black tries to capture the cutting stone in a **ladder*** with 2, White 3 puts two black stones in atari. If he connects at A, Black's formation is totally destroyed by White B.

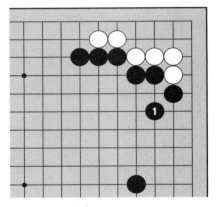

Diagram 5

Diagram 5:

Black 1 is necessary to protect the cutting point. If he reinforces here, Black's wall is invulnerable. The best defense in this formation is the tiger's mouth at Black 1.

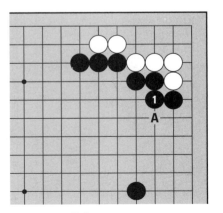

Diagram 6

Diagram 6:

Black 1 also protects the cutting point, but the move at A is preferable, because it does a better job of protecting the right side.

* The ladder is a capturing technique of keeping stones in constant atari and pushing them towards the edge. A discussion of this and other capturing techniques can be found in Volume 1.

Diagram 7:

Black ⬤ has just approached White's formation. Next he intends to invade White's area. Can you guess which spot Black is aiming at?

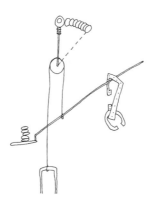

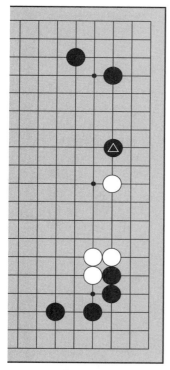

Diagram 7

Diagram 8:

With ⬤, Black intends to invade at 1. Black ⬤ has weakened White considerably; this move along with Black 1 is severe.

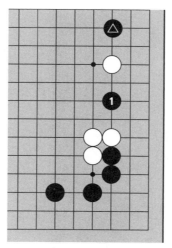

Diagram 8

Diagram 9:

If White plays on top at 2, Black plays at 3. When White continues at 4, Black crosses under with 5. Black has destroyed White's area and made territory as well, so this invasion is a big success.

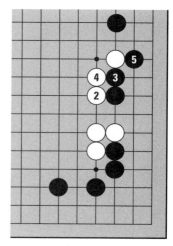

Diagram 9

Diagram 10:

White wants to reinforce as soon as possible. What's the best way? White 1 unquestionably defends against the invasion, but this move is rather passive.

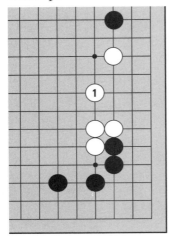

Diagram 10

Diagram 11:

White 1 here is the standard defense. White 1 defends against the invasion at A and also reaches towards the center. As an added bonus, now White has a possible invasion at B.

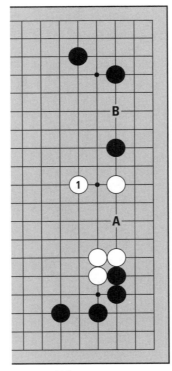

Diagram 11

Diagram 12:

After White ◎, if Black still invades at 2, the invading stones can be surrounded with White 3. If Black tries to get out with 4, White can block at 5. Because of White ◎, the Black stones can't escape.

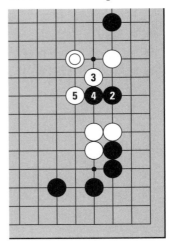

Diagram 12

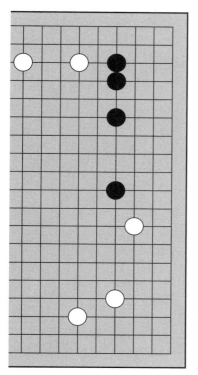

Diagram 13

Diagram 13:

It looks like Black needs to reinforce the upper right side. What do you think?

Diagram 14:

If Black does not reinforce this formation, White may invade at 1. White 1 seems more like an attack on Black ⬤ than an invasion. Because of this weakness, Black would like to reinforce here.

Diagram 15:

What if Black reinforces at 1? The black stones are all securely connected, but this isn't the best defense. White can still come in through the back door at 2.

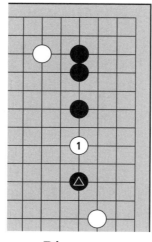

Diagram 14

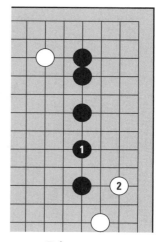

Diagram 15

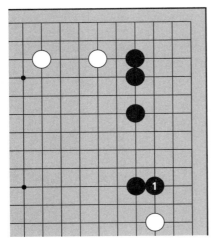

Diagram 16

Diagram 16:

Black 1 here is a good move to protect both weaknesses. Black 1, the so-called iron pillar, is a solid defense move.

Diagram 17:

Because of Black ▲, the invasion at White 1 is foiled by Black 2.

Diagram 18:

If White makes a deep invasion at 1, Black can envelop this stone with 2. The white stone has already been surrounded, and it is almost impossible to live inside. If it can't live, White 1 benefits Black.

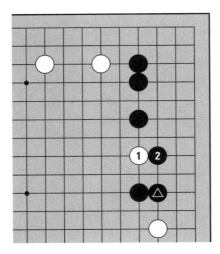

Diagram 17

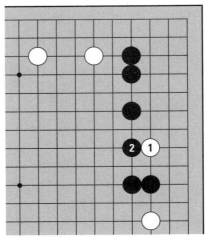

Diagram 18

2. Defense of Weak Stones

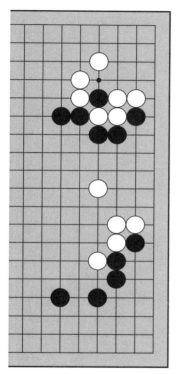

Diagram 19

Diagram 19:

Take a close look at this position. The black stones on the upper right are weak because they have no base. What is the best move to protect them?

Diagram 20:

White can cut at 1 if there is a **ladder breaker** (a white stone along the ladder's path, that prevents Black from capturing). In that case Black cannot play at 2 and then A to capture the cutting stone in a ladder, so he is in big trouble.

Diagram 21:

What if Black connects at 1 to defend the cutting point? Black 1 is a little bit dull. Even though it removes the possibility of being cut, there is a more stylish (that is, efficient) way of connecting.

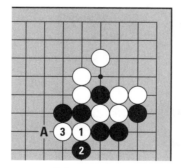

Diagram 20

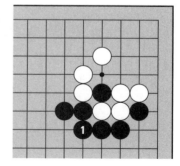

Diagram 21

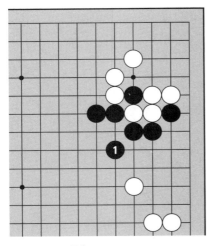

Diagram 22

Diagram 22:

A **tiger's mouth connection** at Black 1 is more active than the solid connection, because it has more scope for running into the center.

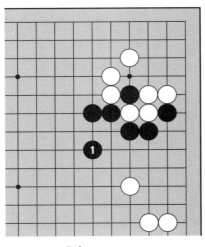

Diagram 23

Diagram 23:

In this case, Black can also defend at 1 here. This formation, called the **knight's move connection**, is even more stylish than the tiger's mouth connection.

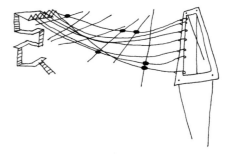

Diagram 24:

One standard pattern results in this formation. Can you find White's weakness? How can you protect it?

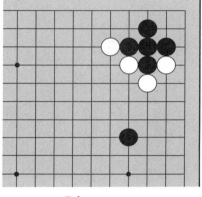

Diagram 24

Diagram 25:

White has two cutting points at A and B, so making the tiger's mouth at 1 is a good defense here.

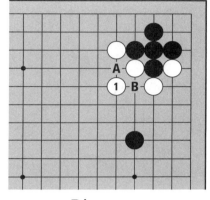

Diagram 25

Diagram 26:

You don't have to be afraid of Black 2. If Black cuts and captures with 2 and 4, White's group is reinforced with 3 and 5. By sacrificing one non-crucial stone, White's formation has become stronger.

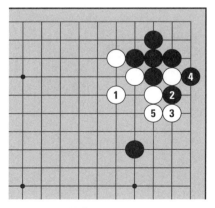

Diagram 26

Diagram 27:

White 1 is not a perfect connection because it leaves an important cutting point at A. Even though Black may not cut at A immediately, leaving this kind of flaw behind is uncomfortable for White. The tiger's mouth connection is a good way to protect two cutting points at once.

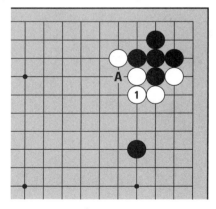

Diagram 27

Diagram 28:

There is a flaw in the black stones' formation—Black is stretched too thin. Try to find a way to protect the cutting point.

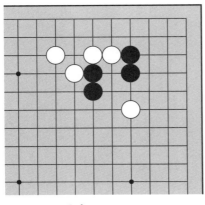

Diagram 28

Diagram 29:

If Black doesn't reinforce here, White pushes up at 1. Black can block at 2, but then White 3 cuts this group in two. With this cut, all the black stones are in danger.

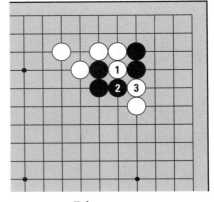

Diagram 29

Diagram 30:

What if Black protects the weak point with a **solid connection** at 1? Once again, there is a more efficient connection.

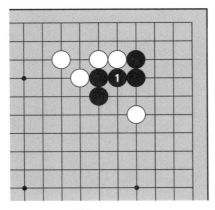

Diagram 30

Diagram 31:

You may recognize from Volume I that in this case, the best connection is the **bamboo joint** of Black 1. If White plays straight down at 2, Black blocks at 3 to make a base in the corner. Black 1 defends both the cutting point and the corner territory.

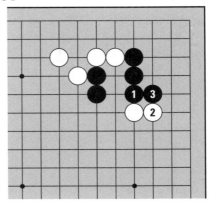

Diagram 31

Diagram 32:

This position is similar to the last diagram, but there is no white stone on the right side. If you want to prevent White from cutting, and defend your territory in harmony with Black , what is the best move?

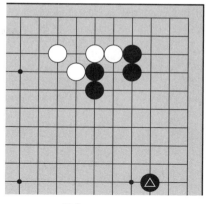

Diagram 32

Diagram 33:

If Black doesn't reinforce here, White can try to penetrate at 1 and then cut at 3. The subsequent difficult fight isn't favorable for Black, so he would like to prepare for the cut at White 3.

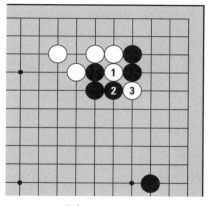

Diagram 33

Diagram 34:

The solid connection at Black 1 certainly settles the question of the cut, but is too one-dimensional. The invasion at A is expected because Black's formation on the right side is too loose.

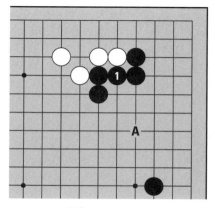

Diagram 34

Diagram 35:

The bamboo joint at Black 1 is more effective, since it protects the cut and helps to defend the area on the right side. However, there is an even better move than making the bamboo joint.

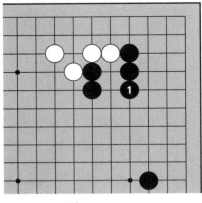

Diagram 35

Diagram 36:

Black 1 is the best defense. It protects the cutting point and does the most to defend Black's area on the right side.

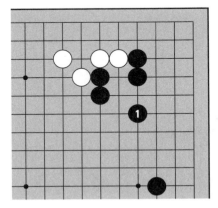

Diagram 36

Diagram 37:

If White tries to penetrate at 2 anyway, Black blocks at 3. Black ⬤ makes a tiger's mouth.

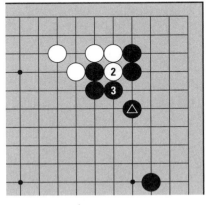

Diagram 37

As you may have gleaned, it's important to defend actively, that is, to play defensive moves that serve more than one purpose.

Go Equipment

Go has been played continuously for 4000 years. In that time, go sets have ranged from the fantastic – boards carved in the shape of giant turtles, with playing pieces (called "stones") made of precious metals and gems – to the understated set of the current century, made of a slab of honey-colored wood and stones of slate and clam shell or glass. A complete go set can be as simple as a board, stones, and bowls. Each of these items can range from a few dollars to hundreds of thousands.

The current style of board comes in two versions: table boards and floor boards. Table boards are meant to sit on a table (hence the name) and range from 1/2" to 2 1/8' thick. They are usually two or more pieces of wood permanently joined (a single piece this thin would tend to warp over time), but the thinner ones may be slotted or hinged to fold in half for more portability. Floor boards have carved wooden legs and stand between 9 and 15 inches high. These are meant to be played on while you sit on a cushion on the floor. The board itself is usually made of a single piece of wood, ranging from 4 1/2" to approximately 8 1/2" thick. On the underside, the thicker boards often have a carved inverted pyramid of unknown symbolism. On the surface, a black grid, usually 19 x 19, is applied with a special ink. Boards with 13 x 13 lines and 9 x 9 lines are also standard. Playing on a smaller grid results in a faster game - a typical 19 x 19 game may last an hour, a 13 x 13 game 30 minutes, and a 9 x 9 game may take 15 minutes.

The best board woods have several distinctive qualities. Most importantly, they have the right kind of color and grain for easy playability. They also have a tiny bit of give, to produce optimal tone when struck with a stone. The wood is soft enough to develop indentations on the playing surface over time.

These days, stones are most often made of glass. They can also be made from white clamshell and black slate. A full set will contain at least 180 opaque white stones and 180 black ones (one for every intersection, save one, on the 19x19 board). It's no problem, though, if you are missing a few. Stones are a little over 2cm in diameter (a little less than an inch) and vary from 6mm to 10mm thick (1/4 to 3/8 inch). In general, thicker stones are more expensive. The most common go-stone shape is biconvex. (Other, less commonly found stones are flat on one side.) Many go aficionados make their own sets, but making the stones these days is a bit extreme - you can get a good set of glass stones for less than $20.

Go bowls can be made of a variety of different woods or plastic, fashioned into bowls in a number of traditional shapes with loosely fitting lids. They come in sets of two matched bowls, interchangeable for the black and white stones.

If you can't find go equipment in your local game store, you can find Samarkand on-line at www.samarkand.net to order from a complete line of boards, stones, bowls, and other go accessories.

10

THE ART OF THE CAPTURING RACE

A capturing race is a fight to block your opponent's liberties (the lines emerging from a stone) before your own liberties are blocked. Whoever has more liberties wins, but there are some important fine points.

1. How to Make More Liberties

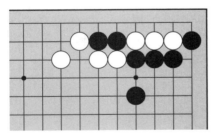

Diagram 1

Diagram 1:

Two black stones and three white stones are involved in a capturing race. Who do you think will win? The two black stones have two liberties. The three white stones have three liberties. White wins the capturing race.

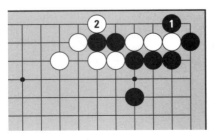

Diagram 2

Diagram 2:

Even if it is Black's turn, this capturing race is in White's favor. If Black blocks a liberty with 1, White can put Black's two stones in atari with 2.

The side that has more liberties wins, but if the sides have the same number of liberties, the side whose turn it is to play wins.

Diagram 3:

Here two black stones and three white stones are in a capturing race. Count the number of liberties and you can predict who will win.

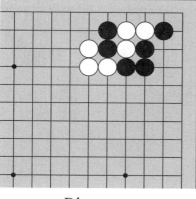

Diagram 3

Diagram 4:

The two black stones have two liberties at A and B. The three white stones have two liberties also, at C and D. Therefore, this capturing race will be won by the side whose turn it is to play.

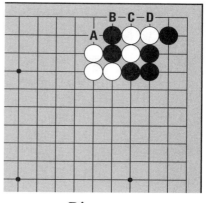

Diagram 4

Diagram 5:

If it's Black's turn, he can put three stones in atari with 1.

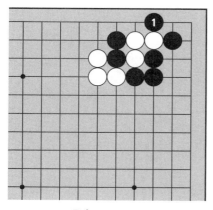

Diagram 5

Diagram 6:

If it's White's turn, she can put two stones in atari with 1.

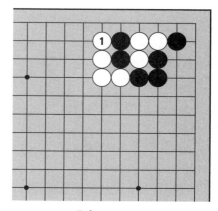

Diagram 6

Sometimes, even though it may appear that you have fewer liberties, you may be able to win a capturing race by gaining more liberties.

Diagram 7:

Black seems to be in danger, because Black has only two liberties to White's three. However, Black can win this capturing race.

Diagram 8:

If Black simply blocks a liberty at 1, White can play atari at 2. To win, Black has to find a way to gain more liberties.

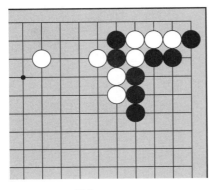

Diagram 7

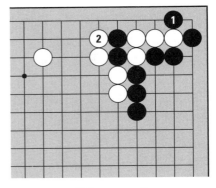

Diagram 8

Diagram 9:

Black 1 is a good move in this case. White has to extend at 2. Black can push again at 3 if he wants before blocking a liberty at 5. By playing at 1, Black has gained an additional liberty, so now he can win this capturing race.

Diagram 10:

What if White blocks at 2 instead? White has a defect in the surrounding wall. Black can play atari at 3, and if White connects at 4, Black catches a stone with 5. There's no hope of White's winning the capturing race now.

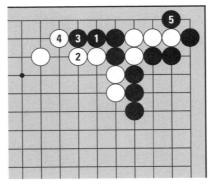

Diagram 9

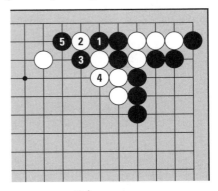

Diagram 10

Diagram 11:

Four black and five white stones are in a capturing race. Black has two liberties and White has three, so it looks like White is sure to win. However, due to a curious feature of the corner, Black can turn the tables.

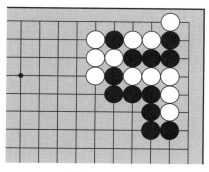

Diagram 11

Diagram 12:

Just blocking a liberty with 1 isn't very useful, because White can play atari with 2.

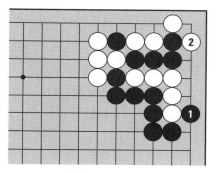

Diagram 12

Diagram 13:

Black 1 is a good move in this case. Do you see why Black can win the capturing race now?

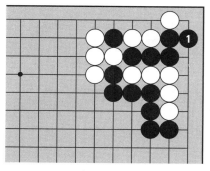

Diagram 13

Diagram 14:

White would like to block a liberty, but has to play at 2 first. (White can't play at A because that would be playing into atari.) Black blocks a liberty with 3. Once again White can't play at A. After 4, White can finally play at A, but Black can play atari first at 5. Because of a strange property of the corner, Black can win this capturing race.

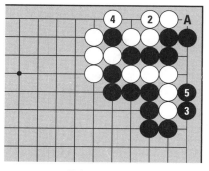

Diagram 14

2. Eye vs. No-eye

There is a big difference between stones that have an eye as a liberty and stones that don't. Even if they have the same number of liberties, the side with an eye captures the side with no eye, regardless of whose turn it is. The Go proverb "one eye beats no eye" refers to this situation, and is very useful to keep in mind.

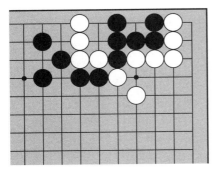

Diagram 15:

Four white stones and six black stones are in a capturing race. Black has three liberties and White has four, but one of Black's liberties is an eye. In this case, Black is sure to win.

Diagram 15

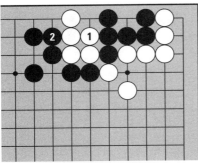

Diagram 16:

White blocks a liberty in vain at 1. Black blocks a liberty at 2.

Diagram 16

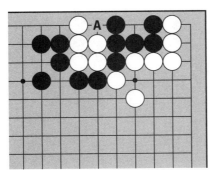

Diagram 17:

If White wants to capture, a stone at A is necessary to put Black in atari, but by playing at A, White is playing into atari. In a capturing race, remember "one eye beats no eye". Keep the proverb in mind and try the following quiz.

Diagram 17

Diagram 18:

In this capturing race between three white stones and four black stones, where should Black play to kill?

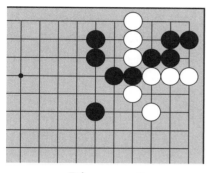

Diagram 18

Diagram 19:

If Black starts the fight by blocking a liberty at 1, the sequence from White 2 to White 6 is the best for both sides. It ends in **dual life** (a situation where both sides live without two eyes), failure for Black in this case.

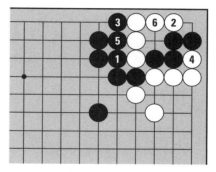

Diagram 19

Diagram 20:

Black 1 is the vital point of the capturing race. Black intends to make this no contest by making one eye. Now the three white stones can be captured.

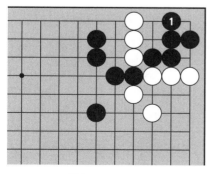

Diagram 20

Diagram 21:

If White starts to block liberties, Black can do the same. Try to confirm for yourself that after making an eye with 1, Black is ahead in this race.

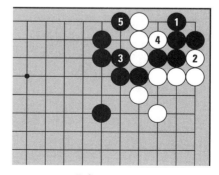

Diagram 21

KO FIGHTING AND KO THREATS

Ko is an interesting, often troublesome fight. As you may have seen in Volume 1, if your opponent captures a stone in ko, you have to use a ko threat before you can return to capture. This isn't an easy matter. This chapter will explain the general technique of ko fighting.

1. Ko Types

There are many types of ko, from kos worth only one point to very large kos on which the game may depend.

Diagram 1:

Take a look at the corner. There is a black stone that can be captured in ko. Let's suppose that White takes the ko.

Diagram 2:

White captures the stone in ko at 1. Even though the white stone is in atari, since it has just captured in ko, Black has to play a ko threat before capturing. On the other hand, Black may not fight the ko at all, because—

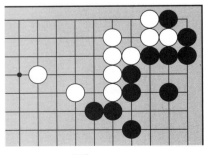

Diagram 1

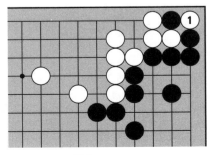

Diagram 2

Diagram 3:

This ko cannot be worth more than one point, very small as moves go. Even if White wins this ko by connecting at 2, it's not particularly painful, so Black doesn't have to fight.

The next example is a different story.

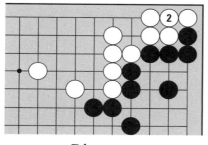

Diagram 3

Diagram 4:

Black and White are tangled in a ko shape. This is a big ko.

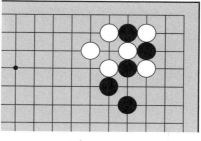

Diagram 4

Diagram 5:

If White wins this ko by capturing at 1, the corner will become solid white territory, approximately a twenty-point gain. Furthermore, White will become strong enough to harass the neighboring black stones. What happens if Black wins the ko?

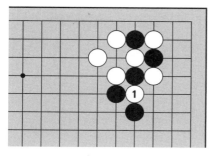

Diagram 5

Diagram 6:

After Black takes the ko, let's suppose he wins this ko and takes a white stone at 2. Now the situation is completely reversed—the corner has become solid black territory. Compare this diagram with **Diagram 5** and you can see the importance of this ko. Whoever wins takes the corner and dominates the countryside.

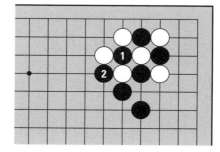

Diagram 6

2. Don't Be Afraid of Ko

Many people are afraid of fighting ko, so if they are confronted with a situation that could become ko, they try to avoid it. This is not a good plan.

Diagram 7:

White has just played atari at 1 in the upper right corner. Ordinarily a stone in atari on the second line like this can just be captured, but in this case because of the ko it's not so cut and dried. How can Black play?

Diagram 8:

Naturally Black wants to take the ko at 1. Black can play here because White did not just capture. Next, if White plays 2, threatening to save the stone on the lower side as a ko threat, and Black responds at 3—

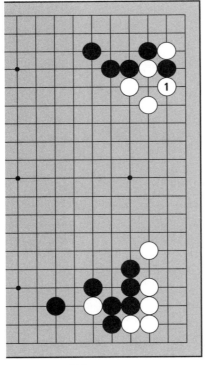

Diagram 7

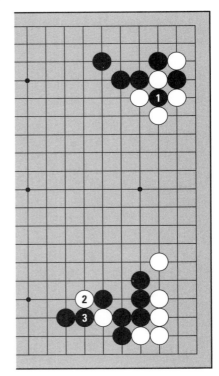

Diagram 8

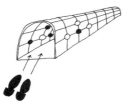

Diagram 9:

White takes the ko with 4. Those who are afraid of ko may play at 5, inducing White 6, but this just leaves a weakness at A while gaining nothing. Being afraid of ko is even worse than fighting and losing. If you don't fight, your opponent wins the ko by default anyway, and you don't get anything in return. Black has to play a ko threat.

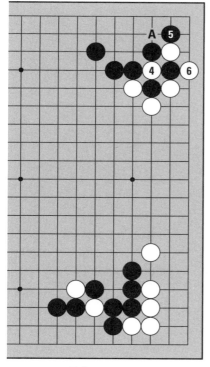

Diagram 9

Diagram 10:

When White takes the ko with 4, Black uses his ko threat at 5. Black 5 is a strong threat, threatening to drive a spike into the white group. In response—

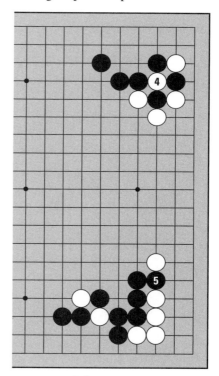

Diagram 10

Diagram 11:

Let's suppose White doesn't respond to the threat and takes at 6. Even though Black lost the ko, he gets even with 7. Black penetrates the lower right corner in compensation for losing the upper right corner. Black 7 in fact kills the group in the lower right corner, so it turns into black territory. Black gained more than he lost. This was a big error on White's part, so—

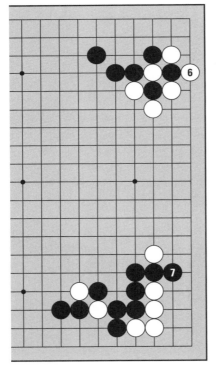

Diagram 11

Diagram 12:

When Black plays the ko threat at 1, White has to respond with 2. Black then takes the ko; if White plays 4 as a ko threat, Black 5 captures.

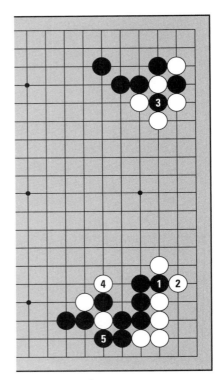

Diagram 12

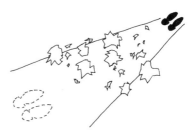

Diagram 13:

When White 6 takes the ko, Black can play 7 as a ko threat. Black lets White engulf this stone, using it as a sacrifice to win the ko. After White 8, Black takes the ko with 9.

Diagram 14:

White has no ko threat now, so she plays an ordinary move at 10. It's not necessary for Black to respond to this move, so he can connect the ko at 11. Black won the ko because he had more ko threats.

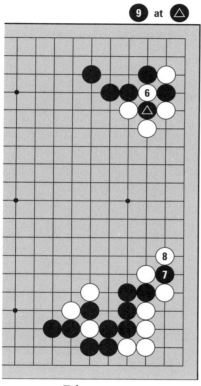

Diagram 13

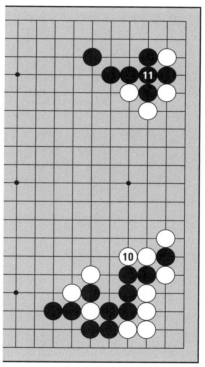

Diagram 14

Consequently, Black has won the large territory in the upper right corner, and the white stones neighboring the strong black wall are nearly useless now. As you have seen, you fight ko by using ko threats. If your opponent doesn't respond to the ko threat, you can still gain by carrying out the threat. Even if you lose the ko, you can be compensated in some other part of the board. So take a deep breath and plunge in. It is not easy to win at go if you are afraid.

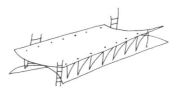

3. How to Use Ko Threats

Whether your opponent will respond to your ko threats is always a great worry. Playing ko threats that your opponent can't ignore is a high-level skill.

Diagram 15:

White 1 captures ko, then Black cuts off a stone at 2. Should White respond to this?

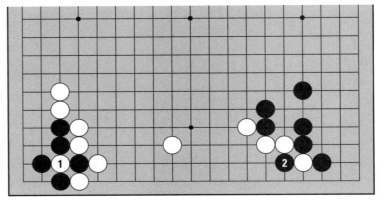

Diagram 15

Diagram 16:

Black's life or death in the lower left corner is dependent on this ko. White doesn't have to respond to Black ◉, so White captures with 3, winning the ko. Black ◉ isn't a good ko threat in this case, because White isn't threatened with heavy losses.

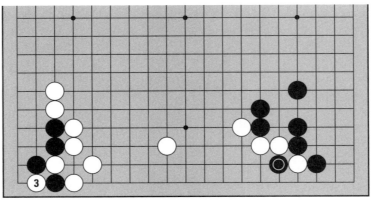

Diagram 16

Diagram 17:

When White takes the ko, Black 2 is a strong ko threat. If White does not respond, Black can kill three stones.

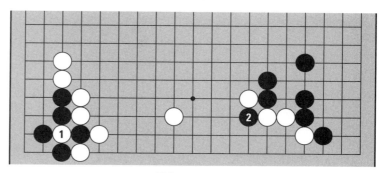

Diagram 17

Diagram 18:

If White captures at 3, winning the ko, Black can play 4, killing the three marked stones. Even though Black lost the ko in the lower left corner, he took a lot of territory on the lower right. The knack of ko fighting is in using "critical" ko threats, so that your opponent feels compelled to respond.

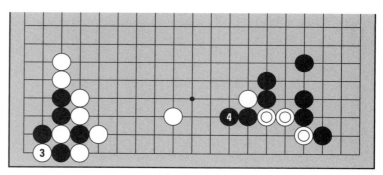

Diagram 18

Diagram 19:

It's a big loss if White doesn't respond to Black 1, so she plays at 2. Then Black can take back the ko with 3.

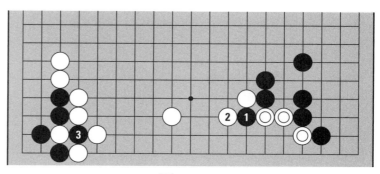

Diagram 19

If Black 1 is used as a ko threat, White feels compelled to respond, so Black can take back the ko. However, you should be careful not to use a ko threat that costs you too much if your opponent does answer it.

Diagram 20:

White captures a stone in ko at 1. If Black loses the ko, his five stones in the corner will be captured. Let's suppose that Black fights this ko.

Diagram 21:

Black 2 threatens to escape from the ladder. White answers at 3. Black 4 takes the ko. Continuing—

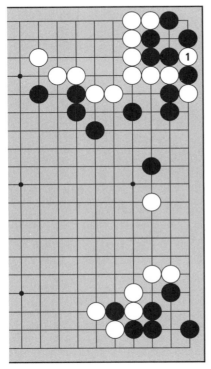

Diagram 20

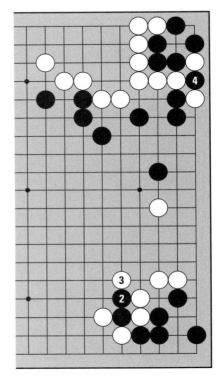

Diagram 21

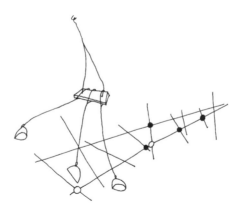

Diagram 22:

White uses 5 as a ko threat. Black 6 is necessary for Black to live. White 7 takes the ko, and then Black tries to escape from the ladder again with 8 as a ko threat.

Diagram 23:

White answers at 9. Black 10 takes the ko and White 11 is used as a ko threat. Black has to make two eyes at 12. It's White's turn to take the ko—

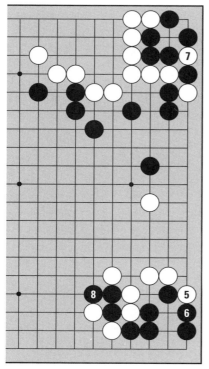

Diagram 22

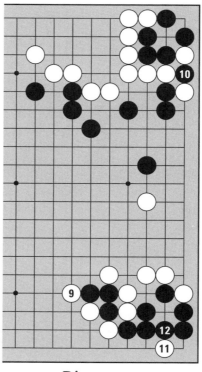

Diagram 23

Diagram 24:

White 13 takes. Black 14 is used as a ko threat; the ladder can be a big source of ko threats. White doesn't have enough ko threats to compete, so she can't win the ko. White 15 answers, and Black takes the ko again with 16.

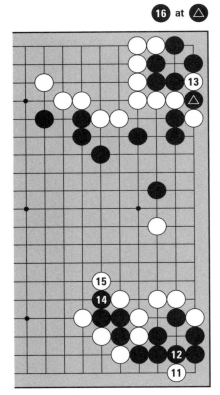

Diagram 24

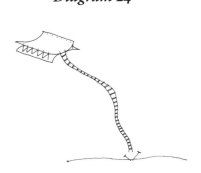

Diagram 25:

White sees that she'll run out of ko threats long before Black does, so she just captures four stones. Black wins the ko by connecting at 18. Is the result a success for Black?

No. Even though Black won the ko, it was not good to increase the number of his stones caught in the ladder. Black sustained heavy damage by the use of costly ko threats. It is not a good plan to use ko threats that do yourself damage. Black should have looked for another ko threat instead of trying to escape from the ladder.

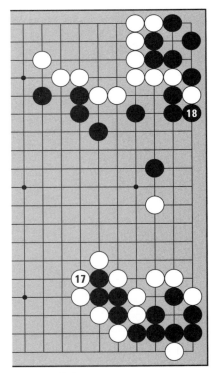

Diagram 25

Go Tournaments

There are two main kinds of Go competitions: various versions of the **knock-out,** where players are eliminated in rounds until the final match, and the **league** or **round robin,** in which each player plays every other player, and the highest scorer is the winner. The winner of a knock-out or a league usually goes on to play the previous year's champion, and is said to be challenging for the title. Since one game may last all day, and the next game may be in a distant city, a Go player with a schedule of seventy or eighty tournament games a year has little time for other activities.

There are also **rating tournaments,** by which professionals are promoted through the ranks to 9 dan, the highest rank, by winning a certain percentage of rated games. Higher-ranked players may skip the early rounds of title tournaments, so most professionals play in the rating tournaments even though they receive little or no compensation.

Titles like the Japanese Honinbo, created in 1603, were held for life by a national Go champion until passed to a son or an adopted son (usually an adopted son, because the title was passed to the top young Go player). Nowadays, Honinbo is the name of one of the annual titles held in Japan, sponsored by a major newspaper. Other titles include the Meijin and the Kisei. Korea and modern-day Japan have a similar system of annual tournaments, with some titles bearing the same name but differing in pronunciation. For example, the Kisei ("Go Sage") is called the Kisung in Korean. China has yet another series of annual tournaments. Players from one association generally are not eligible to play in another associations' tournaments; however, some players, like Cho Hoon-hyun 9-dan, hold membership in both the Korean and Japanese Go Associations.

There are also professional international competitions, to which each association sends representatives. One of the largest, the Ing Cup, has a first prize of US $400,000. A competition to select the North American representative for the Fujitsu Cup, another large international tournament, is held every winter in a different North American city; the public is welcome to observe. Contact the American Go Association for more information.

12

LIFE AND DEATH

The outcome of a game depends upon life and death. It's quite a surprise when stones you thought were alive are killed, or stones you thought you had killed rise from the grave. Let's prevent this kind of surprise in your games by enlarging your knowledge of life and death.

1. The Throw-in

The **throw-in** is a way of killing a group by reducing eye space.

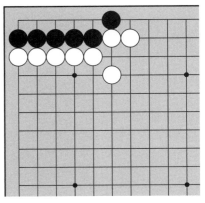

Diagram 1

Diagram 1:

White to play. Let's kill a group of stones.

Diagram 2:

The atari at White 1 lets Black make four points of territory in a line with 2. This group is alive.

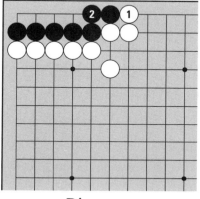

Diagram 2

Diagram 3:

White 1, the throw-in from Volume I, is the right way to kill.

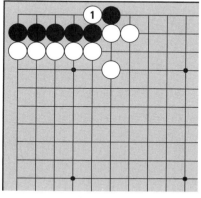

Diagram 3

Diagram 4:

If Black 2 takes a stone, White 3 attacks at the vital center point. This group of stones is now dead. (White ◎ is a false eye.)

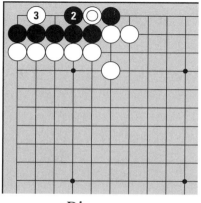

Diagram 4

Diagram 5:

It's also possible to kill the group at White 1. If Black connects at 2, White can prevent this group from making two eyes with 3. (However, White 1 in **Diagram 3** is better, because it removes the possibility of Black's crawling out and connecting to living stones in the future.)

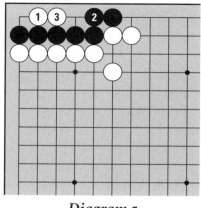

Diagram 5

Diagram 6:

Where should White play to kill this group?

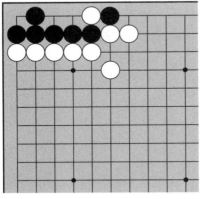

Diagram 6

Diagram 7:

If White takes a stone at 1, Black can make two eyes with 2.

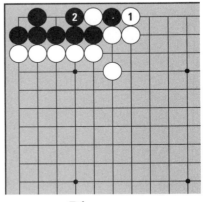

Diagram 7

Diagram 8:

White 1 is the way to kill this group. Even if Black captures two stones with 2—

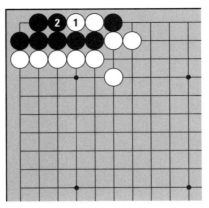

Diagram 8

Diagram 9:

The throw-in at White 3 kills. The throw-in is an enormously useful technique for killing.

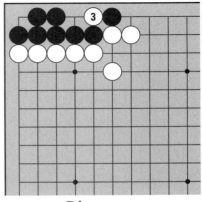

Diagram 9

2. *Dual Life*

As you know, you have to make two separate points of territory, or two eyes, for life. But you can live even without two eyes in the formation called dual life.

Diagram 10:

Black can't make two eyes here because of the white stones inside his group. Nevertheless, Black can't be killed.

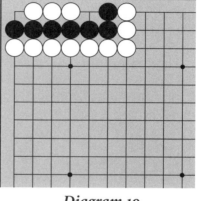

Diagram 10

Diagram 11:

If White tries to take the black stones by playing at 1, four white stones will be in atari and Black can take them off with 2.

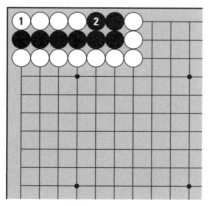

Diagram 11

Diagram 12:

Now Black has four points of territory in a line, so this group is alive.

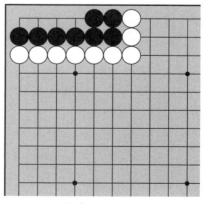

Diagram 12

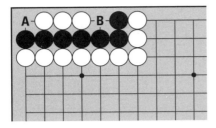

Diagram 13

Diagram 13:

If White tries to kill, Black can live, so White has no choice but to leave the group alone. On the other hand, Black can't take the white stones, because any move here would put his own stones in atari. (Try to confirm this for yourself.) This is dual life. Dual life isn't counted when you finish the game. No stones are removed, and A and B aren't anyone's points.

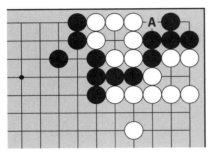

Diagram 14

Diagram 14:

Here is a slightly different example of dual life. Both groups are cut and each has one eye. Even though neither side has two eyes, both sides are alive. Neither side can attack at A, because that would be placing one's own stones in atari.

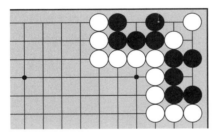

Diagram 15

Diagram 15:

Here Black has one point on either side, but is separated by the two white stones. This shape is also dual life, even though White has no eyes at all.

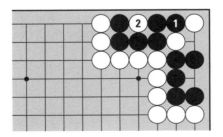

Diagram 16

Diagram 16:

Let's suppose that Black attacks at 1. Then the six black stones are in atari and can be captured by White 2. Once again neither side can play, so both players leave the area alone. At the end of the game, don't count any points for either side, even if one side has an eye and the other does not.

Dual life is not all that common but when you do come across it, remember both sides are alive, and don't count any points in dual life at the end of the game.

3. Eye Shapes

So far, you've learned that in order to live, groups must be able to make two separate points of territory called eyes. In the context of life and death, a group's territory is called **eye space.** Eye space comes in various forms, called **eye shape.** Three points in a line is the eye shape called **straight three**. Four points of territory in an L-shape is called **bent four**. These eye shapes were described in Volume 1, but let's review them here.

Diagram 17:

The eye shape in the upper left corner is straight three, and in the center is bent four. The eye shape in the upper right corner is **straight four**. The eye shape in the lower left corner is **square four**. The eye shape in the lower right corner is called **radial five** (a.k.a. bulky five or the Jeep). Straight three and radial five can live if it is your turn, or be killed if it is your opponent's turn. Straight four and bent four are alive without playing. (There is one exception: the case of bent-four-in-the-corner. Never mind this for now.) The square four can't live no matter what.

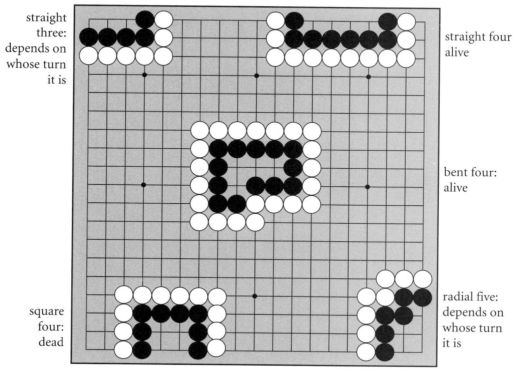

Diagram 17

Diagram 18:

This looks like a bent four, but notice that the Black stones are not all solidly connected to each other. If it is White's turn, this group can be killed.

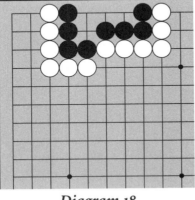

Diagram 18

Diagram 19:

White can atari at 1. When Black connects at 2, White can play at the vital center point of 3. This group is now dead.

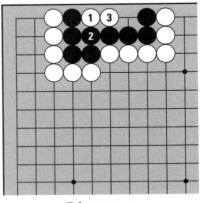

Diagram 19

Diagram 20:

White can kill this group at 1 here too. Try to confirm this for yourself.

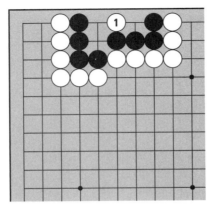

Diagram 20

Diagram 21:

This eye shape looks like bent four, but Black has to reinforce at 1 or A to live. *If the stones in a "living" eye shape are not all solidly connected to each other, **check to make sure** they can't be put into atari, as in Diagram 19.*

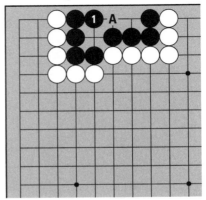

Diagram 21

Let's look at a radial five. Life or death of the radial five depends on whose turn it is to play.

Diagram 22:

Black plays hane (turns the corner) at 1, White blocks at 2, then Black plays hane on the other side with 3. Reducing the opponent's eye space from the outside is a common way to kill a group. When White blocks at 4, the resulting eye shape looks like the radial five. Where is the vital point?

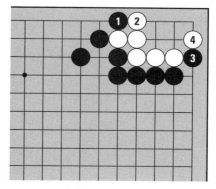

Diagram 22

Diagram 23:

Black 1 is the vital center point. White can't make two eyes or dual life here. If White takes a stone at 2, Black can play at 3. Black ● is a false eye (notice White 2 can be put in atari).

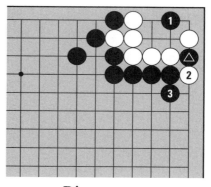

Diagram 23

Diagram 24:

Black shouldn't block at 2. If he does, White can make trouble by cutting at 3. This creates a ko. (Do you see it?) If White wins the ko, the corner group can escape.

So far, we've only looked at eye shapes of less than six points. Let's look at two of the "sixes".

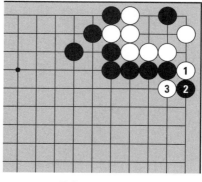

Diagram 24

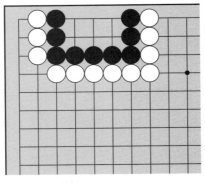

Diagram 25

Diagram 25:

This is **rectangular six.** If it is White's turn, what will happen?

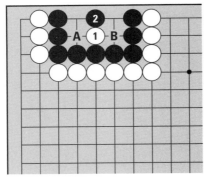

Diagram 26

Diagram 26:

Rectangular six is alive. If White attacks in the middle at 1, Black can live by playing on the "other middle" at 2. If White A, Black B, and if White B, Black A, so Black has two eyes either way.

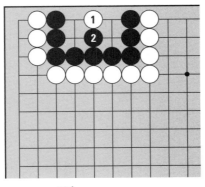

Diagram 27

Diagram 27:

The rectangular six has two center points, so it stands to reason that if White plays one, Black can always play the other. If White attacks at 1 here, Black can play 2.

Diagram 28:

This six-point eye shape is called **flower six** (some people call this "rabbitty six," and then, unfortunately, point out the ears and whiskers).

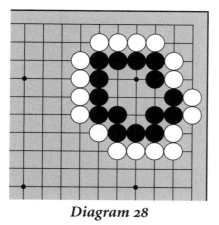

Diagram 28

Diagram 29:

The flower six can be killed by White 1. Black can't make two eyes or even dual life.

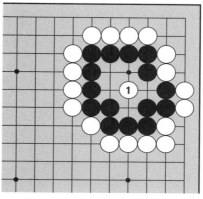

Diagram 29

Diagram 30:

The vital center point of the flower six is White 1 in the previous diagram. Hence, this group has to be reinforced there in order to live. Even though the radial five and the flower six are fairly large eye shapes, they can be captured unless you reinforce them at the vital center point.

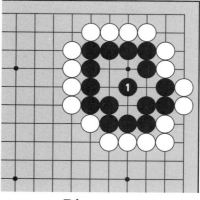

Diagram 30

Eye shapes of seven points or more are large enough to live without reinforcement. However, you have to be careful about possible cutting points and space-reducing moves like the hane and the throw-in.

13

THE ART OF CONTACT FIGHTING

Contact fighting is what it sounds like—a fight in which stones make contact with each other, or generally speaking, moves played on your opponent's liberties. Contact fighting is an integral part of playing go; it's impossible to avoid these complicated, often messy fights.

1.   *The Diagonal Attachment*

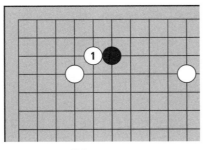

Diagram 1

Diagram 1:

How can Black deal with the **diagonal attachment** of White 1?

Diagram 2:

If Black doesn't respond, the tiger's mouth at White 1 is severe. It's difficult for Black to do anything with his cornered stone, so—

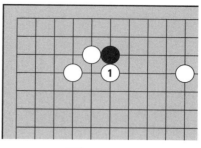

Diagram 2

Diagram 3:

Black 1 is the standard way to cope with the diagonal attachment. It is important not to allow your opponent to form the tiger's mouth shape by playing this point.

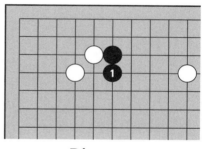

Diagram 3

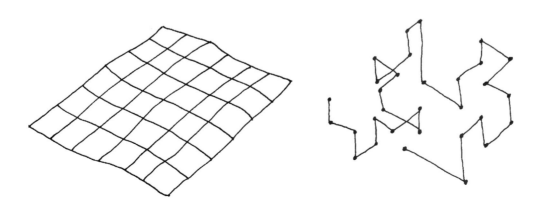

2. *Preventing the Tiger's Mouth*

Diagram 4:

If it's Black's turn, where should he make a move?

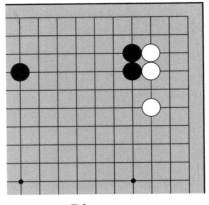

Diagram 4

Diagram 5:

If it's White's turn, the tiger's mouth at White 1 is the vital point. (Hitting the head of two stones like this is also a vital point.)

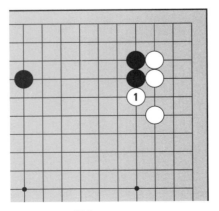

Diagram 5

Diagram 6:

Black 1 is necessary to prevent White from making the tiger's mouth. This move solidifies Black's wall and gives him the opportunity to push in at A.

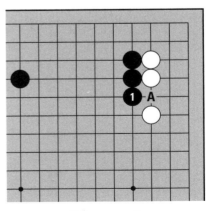

Diagram 6

3. The Head of Two Stones

Diagram 7:

White invaded under the star point stone. Black blocks one side with 2, and White pushes at 3. What should Black do here?

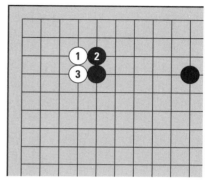

Diagram 7

Diagram 8:

Hitting the head of two stones at 1 is the go player's automatic response. White is forced into pushing from a low position.

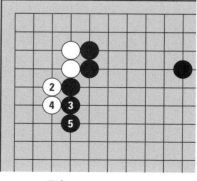

Diagram 8

Diagram 9:

After White 2, Black 3 can just keep going. If White pushes at 4, Black continues at 5, making a strong wall facing the center. This sequence is favorable for Black, because the white group is too low to make as much territory as Black stands to make.

Diagram 9

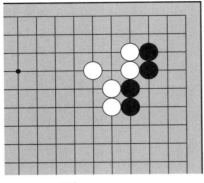

Diagram 10

Diagram 10:

If it's Black to play, where is the key point? Watch out for the hit at the head of two stones.

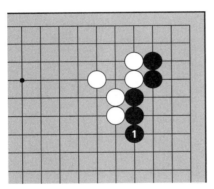

Diagram 11

Diagram 11:

Extending at Black 1 is the most urgent point. Black is developing a formation on the side.

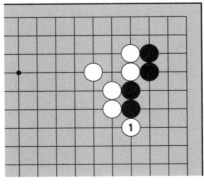

Diagram 12

Diagram 12:

If Black doesn't play here, White will hit the head of two stones at 1, constraining Black's development. Try to be careful not to allow your opponent to hit the head of two stones.

4. *The Triple Approach*

Diagram 13:

White approaches the the corner star point stone with the knight's move on both sides. There is a vital point in this case.

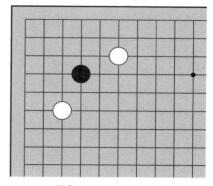

Diagram 13

Diagram 14:

If Black doesn't respond, White's enclosure at 1 is severe. White 1 is a **triple approach,** surrounding Black neatly. If Black tries to escape at 2, White blocks at 3. If Black pushes at 4, White blocks at 5. It's dangerous to be surrounded like this.

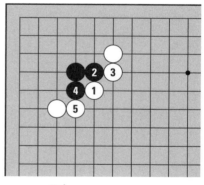

Diagram 14

Diagram 15:

Black 1 heads off the potential siege, marching out to the center of the board. Later Black may get an opportunity to attack White's approach stones. When you can be surrounded with just one move, it's very important to get out while you can.

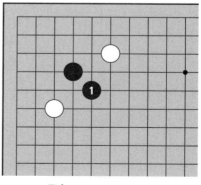

Diagram 15

5. Preventing the Spike

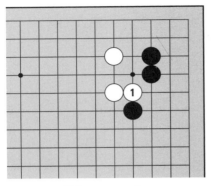

Diagram 16

Diagram 16:

If White makes a move at 1, what should Black do?

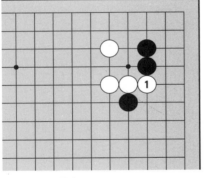

Diagram 17

Diagram 17:

Black has to defend. If White cuts at 1, Black's territory will be destroyed and his group cut in two. Don't let your opponent drive a **spike** through your stones like this.

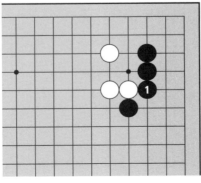

Diagram 18

Diagram 18:

Black 1 is essential to keep the side territory and to protect his stones.

Diagram 19:

If White pushes in at 1, what should Black do?

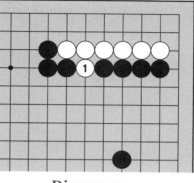

Diagram 19

Diagram 20:

If Black doesn't block, White will come out at 1. It's not good to allow your wall to be broken through like this.

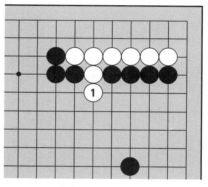

Diagram 20

Diagram 21:

Black 1 is indispensible to defend this area. If this wall is breached, Black's strategy in this area is a failure.

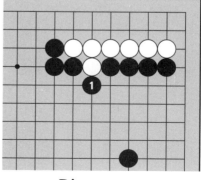

Diagram 21

6. Defending the Weak Point

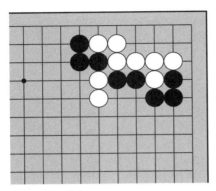

Diagram 22

Diagram 22:

If you look closely, you will find that Black has a serious weak point. How should he protect it?

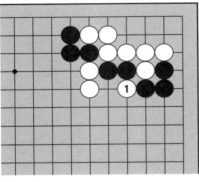

Diagram 23

Diagram 23:

Black's weak point is at White 1, which cuts off two stones. If these two stones are captured, Black's chances of winning this game are slim, because the two white stones floating in the middle of the board spring back into action. Therefore, Black needs to protect this weak point.

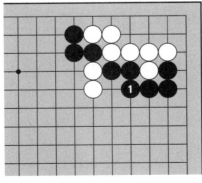

Diagram 24

Diagram 24:

Black 1 certainly saves the two stones, but there is a more efficient way of connecting.

Diagram 25:

The tiger's mouth at Black 1 is not so good in this case because of White's clever play at 2. White can capture two stones in a **snapback*** at 3, so Black has to connect at 3. Black has allowed White to get in another stone at 2, helping her stones in the center.

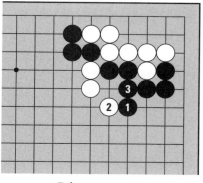

Diagram 25

Diagram 26:

Black 1 is the best way to prevent White from taking advantage of the weak point.

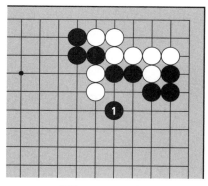

Diagram 26

Diagram 27:

If White pushes at 2, Black will expand the area on the side with 3. If White A, Black B, so the connection is safe.

Compare each kind of connection and try to see for yourself why Black 1 in Diagram 26 is best. Keep it in mind for use in your own games.

* The snapback is a capturing technique using the throw-in, discussed in Volume 1.

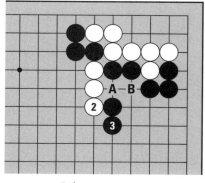

Diagram 27

7. The Peep

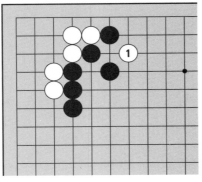

Diagram 28

Diagram 28:

White 1 peeps at Black's tiger's mouth. What is the purpose of this move? How should you respond?

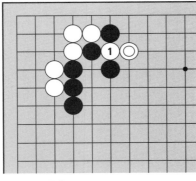

Diagram 29

Diagram 29:

White ◎ is a threat to cut the tiger's mouth connection. If Black does not respond, White will carry out the threat at 1.

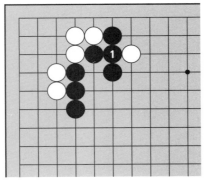

Diagram 30

Diagram 30:

Black should just connect here at 1.

8. *Watch Your Cutting Points*

Diagram 31:

When Black pushes at 1, White needs to be careful to avoid disaster. One needs to be cool and collected enough to defend when necessary.

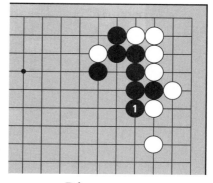

Diagram 31

Diagram 32:

If you were White, would you feel like making a tiger's mouth at White 1? This looks good, but now White's territory can be destroyed with the atari at 2. If White connects at A, Black can catch a stone (and the whole corner in the process) with B.

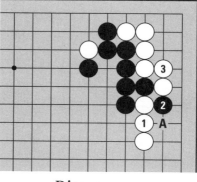

Diagram 32

Diagram 33:

White needs to play at 1 instead. If Black 2, White can connect at 3 or atari at A with no problem. It's important to think of your own weaknesses first.

Diagram 33

9. The Attachment

Diagram 34:

White attaches at 1. What is a good response?

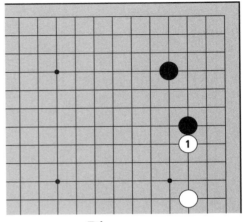

Diagram 34

Diagram 35:

There is a proverb: "Attach, hane." The proverb can be directly applied in this example. When White attaches, Black plays the hane at 1. If White pulls back at 2, Black connects at 3. Black's formation here is pretty good. (If White cuts at 3 instead, it's Black's turn in an even fight, so he should still have the upper hand.)

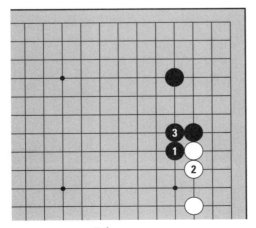

Diagram 35

Diagram 36:

If Black does not respond to the attachment, White plays the hane, Black pulls back at 2, then White connects at 3. White's group has developed nicely, in contrast to the previous diagram.

Moral: it's a good idea to respond to the attachment.

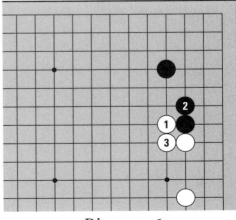

Diagram 36

10. *Defense of Weak Points*

Diagram 37:

White moves out from the corner with 1. White has reinforced, so the Black position is correspondingly weakened. Where is Black's weak point?

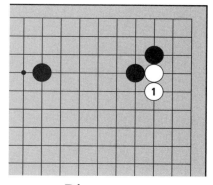

Diagram 37

Diagram 38:

Black has to protect the cutting point by connecting at 1. Later, Black may have the opportunity to attack the two white stones at A.

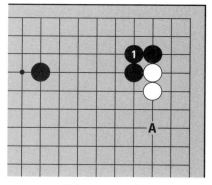

Diagram 38

Diagram 39:

If Black does not defend, these stones will be in trouble if White cuts at 1. If Black tries to drive the cutting stone to the edge, White escapes with 3. Black can't capture White 1, so the corner stone is isolated without any eyes. Connecting is indispensible to prevent the corner territory from changing hands.

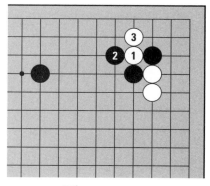

Diagram 39

11. Crosscutting

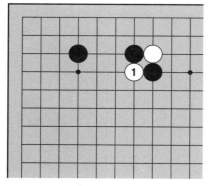

Diagram 40

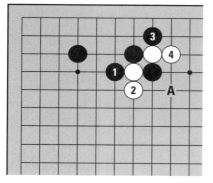

Diagram 41

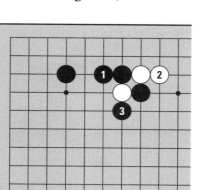

Diagram 42

Diagram 40:

White crosscuts two black stones at 1. This generates a fight. If Black cannot deal with this fight properly, the corner will be seriously damaged.

Diagram 41:

What if Black plays atari at 1? Then White will run at 2. If Black plays atari at 3, White runs at 4. It does not appear that Black's efforts with 1 and 3 are getting anywhere. In fact, White can trap a stone in a **net*** at A.

Diagram 42:

Black 1 is a better response. If White extends at 2, Black can capture a stone in a ladder with 3. This fight led to a nice result for Black.

Moral: **when you are crosscut, often the best response is to extend.** Abuse of the atari tends to spoil your game.

* The net is a capturing technique of blocking the opponent's escape routes, discussed in Volume 1.

12. Aim at Defects

Defense of your own weaknesses is crucial in contact fighting. By the same token, if your opponent ignores weaknesses, you can get a good result by attacking.

Diagram 43:

Three white stones are surrounded. However, the surrounding black group has a defect. By attacking at the weakness, White can live.

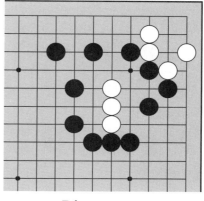

Diagram 43

Diagram 44:

White can cut at 1. This is Black's weak link.

Diagram 45:

If Black connects at 2, White can live by catching a stone at 3. Escaping from a siege like this is a great achievement. The road to success is to take advantage of your opponent's defects.

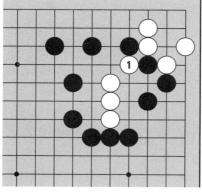

Diagram 44

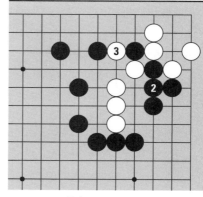

Diagram 45

14

ENDING THE GAME

The endgame is the stage of finishing borderlines. After the middle game, territories are pretty much formed, but they are not solidified yet. As there's little opportunity to recover from mistakes in the endgame, this stage is often decisive.

Diagram 1:

This is a section of a game in the endgame stage. You can tell where Black's and White's territories are, but the borderlines are not yet complete. If it's her turn, White will play as in the next diagram.

Diagram 2:

White plays hane at 1, Black blocks, and White connects. Next Black has to protect the cutting point at 4. White plays hane on the other side with 5, Black blocks, and White connects. Once again Black has to defend the weak point at 8. The borderlines of the corner territory are now complete.

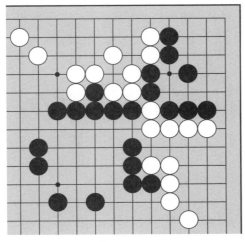

Diagram 1

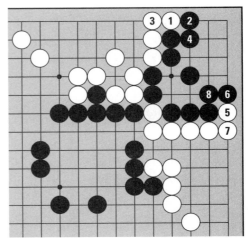

Diagram 2

1. Ending

Go is a game of priorities. The order of the endgame is also determined by priorities, in that you want to play the biggest moves first. What is a "big" endgame move?

Diagram 3:

Depending on whose turn it is to play, there is a big "swing" in the territory in the corner.

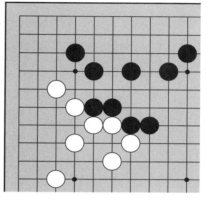

Diagram 3

Diagram 4:

If it's his turn, Black 1 is a good endgame move. An extensive corner is now in Black's possession.

Diagram 5:

If it's her turn, White can slip into the corner with 1. Now the corner turns into White's territory. Black 1 in **Diagram 4** and White 1 here are big endgame.

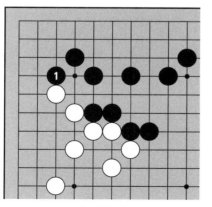

Diagram 4

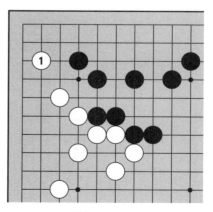

Diagram 5

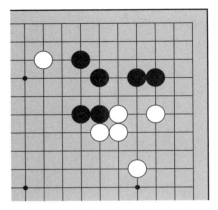

Diagram 6

Diagram 6:

In the middle game, territorial borderlines generally stop at the third line from the edge, as in this diagram.

What It Means: there's a lot of endgame on the second line.

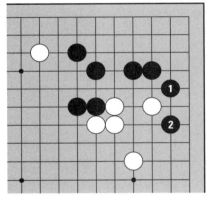

Diagram 7

Diagram 7:

If it's Black's turn, the diagonal at 1 is big. If White does not respond, Black can destroy her territory by jumping in at 2. So—

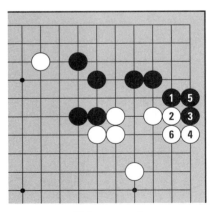

Diagram 8

Diagram 8:

If Black plays at 1, White needs to block at 2 to protect this territory. Black keeps the initiative with 3 and 5.

The Meaning of Sente

The Japanese word *sente* (*sunsoo* in Korean, literally, "leading move" or "first hand") is one of the most used, and most difficult, concepts in Go. Even top players, who understand what sente is and how it works, cannot always recognize it on the battlefield.

The word sente is defined as the initiative, or the opportunity to play anywhere you like (notice you don't keep the initiative if, after playing where you like, you respond to your opponent's response). However, depending on how it is used in conversation, different aspects of the definition are emphasized. **Having** sente means that you have the opportunity to play anywhere you like. **Taking** sente means that rather than responding to your opponent's move, you play where you would like to play. If a move **is** sente, your opponent needs to respond, and if a move **is not** sente, it means your opponent doesn't need to respond. However, one problem of using the word in these narrow senses is that since you can play or not play anywhere you like, "sente" moves may become "not sente" if your opponent doesn't respond to them. Are they really sente or not? This is one of the central questions we are trying to answer as we play go.

Another difficulty is that the idea of "responding" is not very clear—which moves are responses and which moves aren't? Generally, a move isn't a "response" just because it's played in the same area as the last move; a move is a response if it is defensive, passive, or forced in some way. Because go is an additive game, just defending is not enough to pull ahead. So sente carries a kind of emotional connotation—if you feel like you're being led around the board, you're probably a) not taking sente and b) losing. On the other hand, if you get to play everywhere you want, while your opponent struggles to keep up, you're getting a firsthand look at the power of sente.

The word gote (*husoo* in Korean, literally, "following move" or "second hand") is the other side of the coin: imprecisely, a move that your opponent doesn't have to answer, or losing the initiative. Sente is good and gote is bad, but into each life a little gote must fall.

Note: the final "e" in the romanization of Japanese words is pronounced:

sente = SEN-tay

gote = GO-tay

hane = HA-nay

Diagram 9:

If it is White's turn, the diagonal at 1 is big.

Diagram 10:

If Black doesn't respond, White jumps in the corner territory with 2. If Black pushes in at 3, White can cross under at 4. Black has lost a lot of territory.

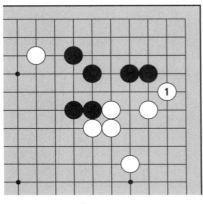

Diagram 9

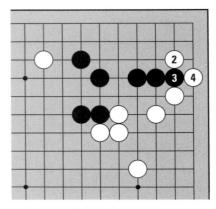

Diagram 10

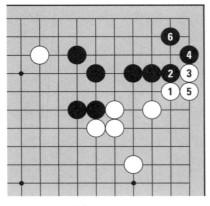

Diagram 11

Diagram 11:

So, after White 1, Black 2 is indispensible to keep the corner. White can now play the hane at 3. Compare this result with ***Diagram 8***. The final size of these territories depends on who plays first (whoever has the initiative makes three points and reduces the opponent's territory by three points). It's important to play this kind of **sente endgame** as soon as possible, before your chance is lost.

White 1 is called sente endgame because after Black responds, White still has the initiative and can grab another endgame move.

If White has to answer Black 2 with a defensive play, Black can take the initiative and play whatever endgame move he wants. We say in this case "White lost sente," "Black now has sente," or "White's move was gote."

Don't worry if you don't get these concepts completely right now—they take time.

2. Shapes to Watch Out For

There are many common endgame sequences, for example, the "hane-block-connection" on the first line from Volume I. However, the endgame is not the time to go on automatic pilot.

Diagram 12:

White played the hane on the first line at 1. How does Black answer?

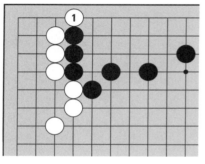

Diagram 12

Diagram 13:

Black should block at 2. White connects at 3, and Black connects at 4. The borderline of this territory is determined without incident. Instead of Black 4—

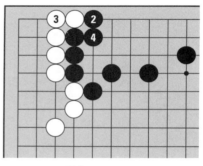

Diagram 13

Diagram 14:

Black can also connect with a tiger's mouth at 1. Either connection is fine. The next example is a bit different.

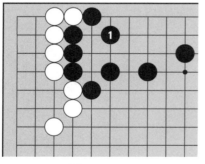

Diagram 14

Diagram 15:

White plays the hane at 1. How should Black answer here?

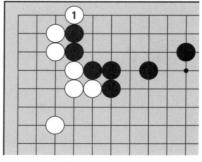

Diagram 15

Diagram 16:

The block at 2 here isn't good because of White 3.

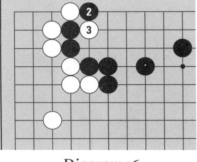

Diagram 16

Diagram 17:

If Black captures a stone at 4, White can cut off two stones at 5. These stones are now in atari and can't escape, so Black has suffered a big loss. Black has to be careful when White plays hane on the first line. (You may notice that in this case, the hane hits the head of two stones.)

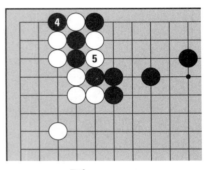

Diagram 17

Diagram 18:

When White plays the hane at 1, giving a bit of ground with Black 2 is necessary.

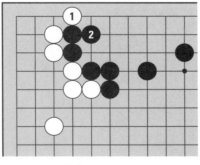

Diagram 18

Diagram 19:

Next if White pushes in at 3, now Black can block at 4. White connects at 5, and Black connects at 6. The borderline is now complete. If there is a cutting point on the borderline, you have to be careful or you may lose your territory.

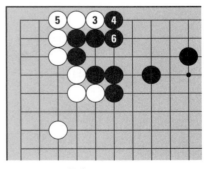

Diagram 19

Diagram 20:

If you look at Black's territory in the corner, you can see a cutting point at A. Does Black need to defend?

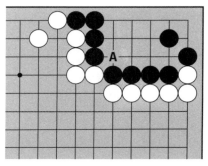

Diagram 20

Diagram 21:

Of course, connecting at 1 is the sure thing. But if the connection isn't necessary, you wouldn't want to put a stone in your own territory, losing one point.

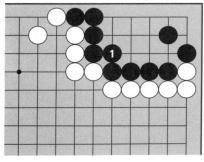

Diagram 21

Diagram 22:

Suppose Black does not defend, and White cuts at 1.

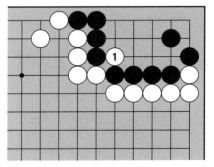

Diagram 22

Diagram 23:

If Black plays the atari at 2, White can come out at 3. The four black stones on the left can now be captured.

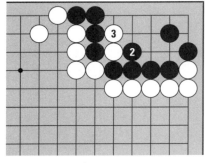

Diagram 23

Diagram 24:

But, when White cuts at 1, Black can play the other atari at 2 here.

Diagram 25:

If White comes out at 3, Black can continue at 4. If White comes out again at 5, connecting at 6 leads to the capture of three white stones. Therefore White 1 is not a threat, so Black doesn't have to defend this cutting point.

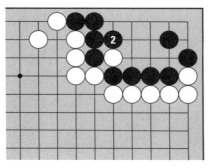

Diagram 24

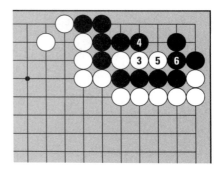

Diagram 25

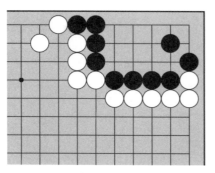

Diagram 26

Diagram 26:

So Black can leave this group as it is. Even though White can cut, Black can capture the cutting stone, so this is not a real defect. This territory is complete as it stands, without connecting. If you can neutralize any attack, you don't need costly defense. But if you can't, you need reinforcement. This requires **reading**, or anticipating a sequence.

Diagram 27:

This position is similar to the last example, but this time, the borderline has a critical defect.

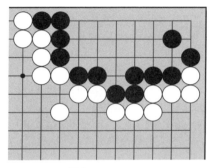

Diagram 27

Diagram 28:

White can cut at 1. Black plays the atari at 2, but when White comes out at 3, now two black stones are in atari.

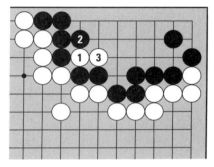

Diagram 28

Diagram 29:

If Black connects the two stones at 4, White 5 can turn and engulf five black stones. Disaster.

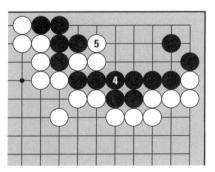

Diagram 29

Diagram 30:

In this case, connecting the defect at Black 1 is indispensible. Otherwise, White can go on a rampage. You must reinforce real defects before you can lay claim to territory.

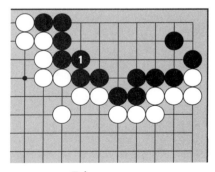

Diagram 30

Synthesis

syn·the·sis: **1.a.** The combining of separate elements to form a coherent whole. **b.** The whole so formed. **2.** Philos. **a.** Reasoning from the general to the particular; logical deduction. **b.** The combination of thesis and antithesis in the dialectical process, producing a new and higher form of being. **3.** Go **a.** Try it yourself. Twenty-five questions covering the material in this book.

Try to answer each question before turning the page. When you see the answer, if your reasoning is different from mine, you may wish to review the pages noted or your transformation process will not be complete. Here's a chart to assess your score:

Multiply the number of questions you answered correctly by four.

above 80:

excellent

52-80:

good

36-48:

average

20-32:

need a little practice

below 20:

please review Volume II again before moving on to Volume III

Question 1:

Whose opening is better?

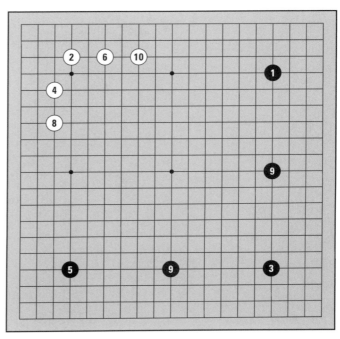

Question 1

Question 2:

White has built an extensive framework in the upper left corner. Can Black contest this area or will it all become White's territory?

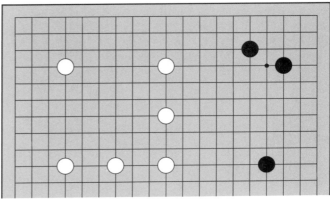

Question 2

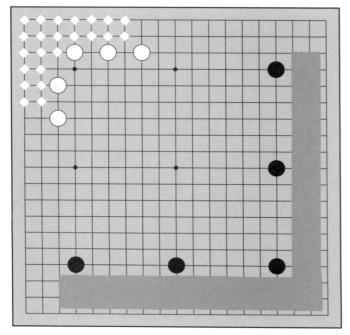

Answer 1

Answer 1:

White has made twenty-odd points of territory, but Black has staked out much more potential territory in this opening, so he is doing better. Following up with good play in the middle and endgame, the shaded area should become much more than twenty points. (pp. 3-5)

Note that it is not because Black's stones are on the fourth line from the edge, and White's are on the third line, that Black is better: it's because his stones are more efficiently spaced to maximize territory-making prospects.

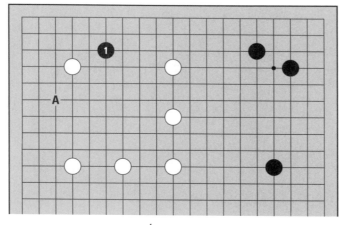

Answer 2

Answer 2:

If Black invades at 1 or at A, it's difficult for White to kill this stone, so this area is still vulnerable. (pp. 6-8)

Question 3:

White plays the endgame move at 1. Where should Black answer?

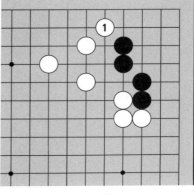

Question 3

Question 4:

What are the three basic rules of the opening?

1. Start _____

2. Next, _____

3. Use _____

Question 5:

What are two main ways to enclose a corner from the 3-4 point?

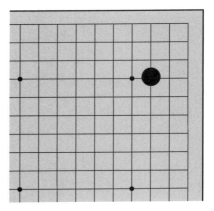

Question 5

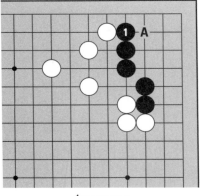

Answer 3

Answer 3:

Black needs to block at 1. If not, White can jump in at A and destroy the corner territory. Additionally, the black stones have lost their base, so their future is uncertain. (p. 9)

Answer 4:

Clueless with that big open board in front of you? (pp. 11-16)

1. Start from the corners.
2. Next, go to the sides.
3. Use the third and fourth lines.

Answer 5a:

Black 1 is a knight's move enclosure. (pp. 18-20)

Answer 5b:

Black 1 here is a one-point enclosure. (pp. 18-20)

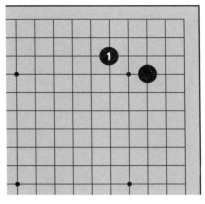

Answer 5a

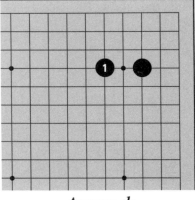

Answer 5b

Question 6:

What are two main ways to approach a corner star point?

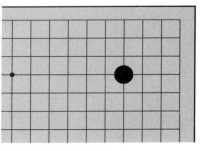

Question 6

Question 7:

What's an appropriate extension from White ◎?

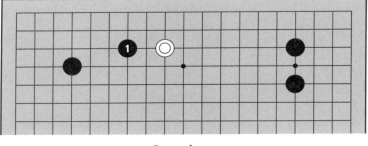

Question 7

Question 8:

What are the six basic *haengma*, or relationships between two stones?

Answer 6a:

White 1 is the knight's move approach. (p. 21)

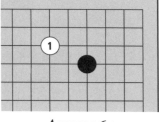

Answer 6a

Answer 6b:

White 1 here is the one-point approach. (p. 21)

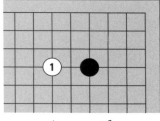

Answer 6b

Answer 7:

From the lone marked stone, White 2, a two-point extension, is an appropriate way make a base in response to Black's attack at 1. (pp. 30-32)

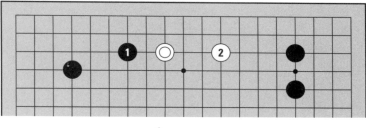

Answer 7

Answer 8:

From left to right, Black stretches, plays the diagonal, the one-point jump, the knight's move, the two-point jump, and the large knight's move. (pp. 38-43)

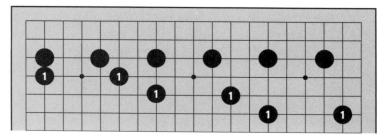

Answer 8

Question 9:

It seems dangerous to invade the upper left side, so instead Black wants to reduce it. Where is the best point to make a shoulder-hit reduction?

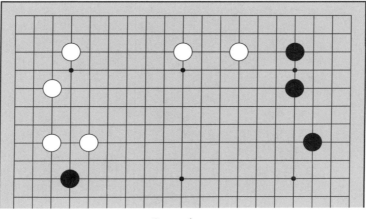

Question 9

Question 10:

Three black and two white stones are in a capturing race. If it's Black to play, how can he capture?

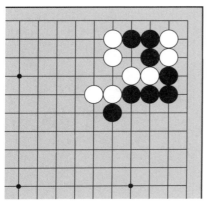

Question 10

Question 11:

Four white and three black stones are in a capturing race in the corner. What is the point both sides need to win?

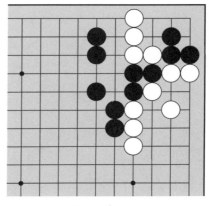

Question 11

Answer 9:

Black 1 is the move. This shoulder hit is the vital point for reduction. (pp. 48-49)

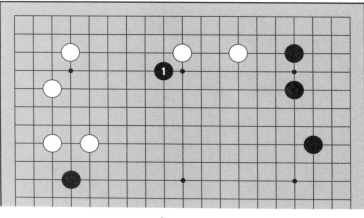

Answer 9

Answer 10:

Black can capture two stones with 1. If White 2, Black 3. Black has one more liberty. (pp. 82-85)

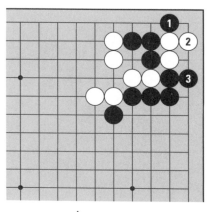

Answer 10

Answer 11:

Black 1 makes an eye. In a capturing race, one eye usually beats no eyes, as in this case. If White plays at 1 first, White can capture. (pp. 86-87)

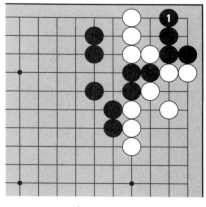

Answer 11

Question 12:

White captures a stone in ko at 1. If Black loses this ko fight, the corner group can be captured. Where is a good ko threat? Try to find a move in the lower right corner that White should answer.

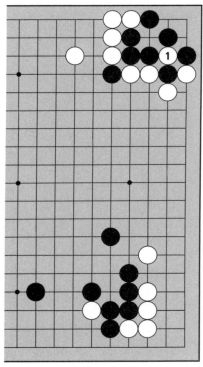

Question 12

Question 13:

Black 1 captures a stone in ko, This ko is very important for both sides. If White plays the dull move at 2 as a ko threat, what should Black do?

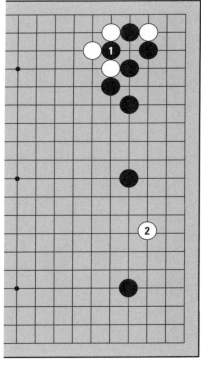

Question 13

Answer 12:

Black has a good ko threat at 1. If White does not answer but instead captures at 2, Black can drive a spike through White's group with 3. If White answers the ko threat at 3 instead of capturing at 2, Black will take back the ko. (p. 92)

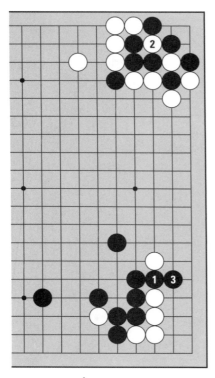

Answer 12

Answer 13:

Black should capture at 1, winning the ko. There's no compelling need to answer White ◎, so it was not a very good ko threat. (p. 94)

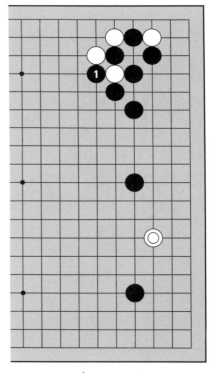

Answer 13

Question 14:

If it is White's turn, she can kill this group. Where is the vital point?

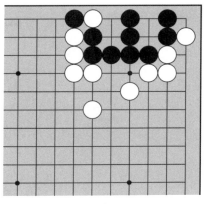

Question 14

Question 15:

The corner looks like Black territory, but if it is White's turn, she can make dual life. How?

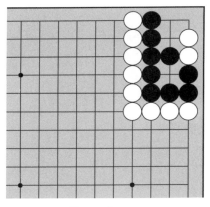

Question 15

Question 16:

Black can't make two eyes, but there is a chance to make dual life. How?

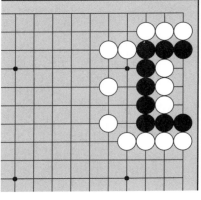

Question 16

Answer 14:

White 1 is the vital point. If Black 2 captures two stones, White can kill by playing the throw-in at White ◎. (pp. 100-102)

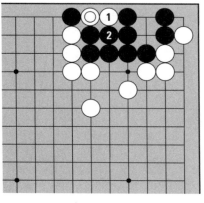

Answer 14

Answer 15:

White 1 makes dual life. If so, neither side has any territory in this area. (pp. 103-104)

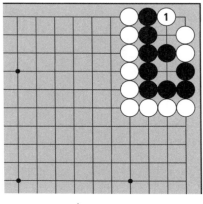

Answer 15

Answer 16:

Black 1 is the vital point to make dual life. Now neither side can be captured in this position. (pp. 103-105)

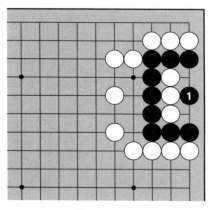

Answer 16

Diagram 1:

The black group cannot be captured even if all its outside liberties are blocked. If White attacks at A, Black can capture at B, (likewise White B, Black A), making the bent four eye shape.

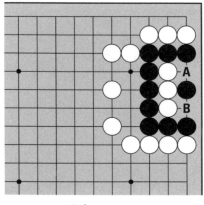

Diagram 1

Question 17:

White has the radial five eye shape. If it's Black's turn, he can kill this group. Where is the vital point?

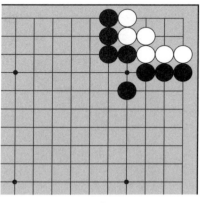

Question 17

Question 18:

White plays the hane at 1. How can Black live?

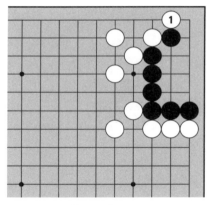

Question 18

Question 19:

Black has a six-point eye shape. This is the flower six, so if it is White's turn, she can kill. Where is the vital point?

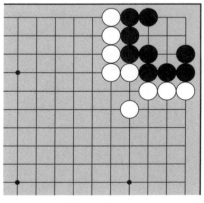

Question 19

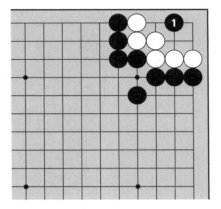

Answer 17

Answer 17:

White's group can be killed by an attack at the vital center point. (p. 107)

Answer 18:

Black 1 is the only move that makes a living formation. (p. 108)

Answer 19:

The Black group can be killed by an attack at the vital center point. (p. 109)

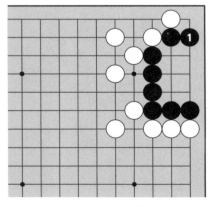

Answer 18

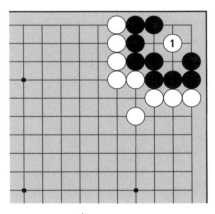

Answer 19

Question 20:

Black played the approach at 1, and White played the diagonal at 2. What should Black do?

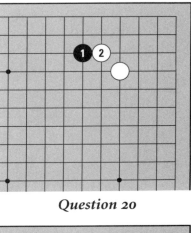

Question 20

Question 21:

White to play. Both sides have a vital point. Where is it?

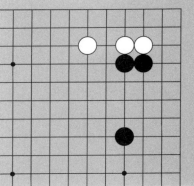

Question 21

Question 22:

Black to play. There's a place that urgently needs reinforcement. Where is it?

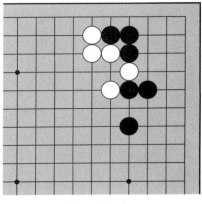

Question 22

Answer 20:

Extending at Black 1, preventing White's tiger's mouth, is the best move. If Black misses this move, a white play at 1 is excellent. (p. 111)

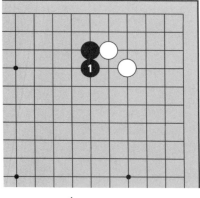

Answer 20

Answer 21:

The tiger's mouth at 1 is the vital point. Hitting the head of two stones like this is very good, so Black should have played at 1 first. (p. 112)

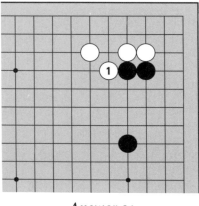

Answer 21

Answer 22:

Blocking at 1 is urgent. (pp. 116-117)

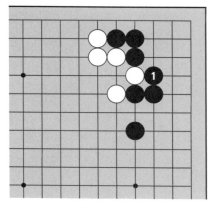

Answer 22

Diagram 2:

If Black does not block, White can drive a spike in at 1, destroying Black's territory. Additionally, Black's stones in the corner are in trouble.

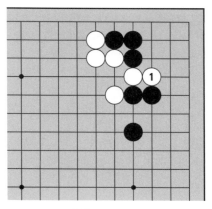

Diagram 2

Question 23:

White attaches under the star point stone at 1. What is the standard way to answer? Try to keep the territory in the corner.

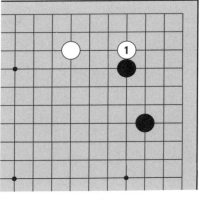

Question 23

Question 24:

Both sides' territory is almost determined, but the corner remains unsettled. Where is the big endgame point for Black?

Question 25:

White to play. Try to find a good endgame move, reducing Black's territory in the corner while increasing White's territory on the side.

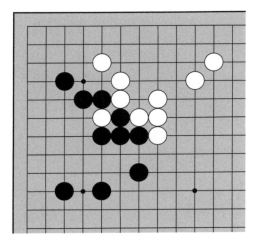

Question 24

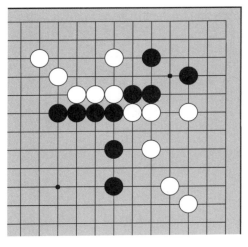

Question 25

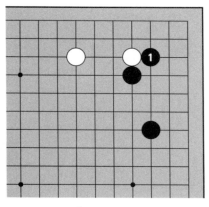

Answer 23

Answer 23:

Black 1 is standard – "if attach, hane." The hane on this side blocks the corner to keep the territory there. (p. 122)

Answer 24:

Black 1 is an enormous endgame move, securing the entire corner. (p. 127)

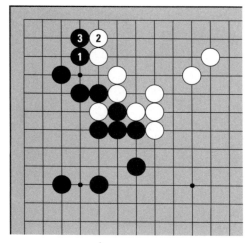

Answer 24

Diagram 3:

If Black misses this move, White can play at 1. The result is the opposite of the previous diagram—the corner becomes White's territory.

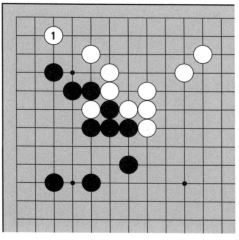

Diagram 3

Answer 25:

If White plays the big sente endgame moves at 1 or 3, Black needs to passively block at 2 and 4. Later White can play the hane-block-connection on the first line, so Black's corner territory is considerably reduced. (pp. 128, 130)

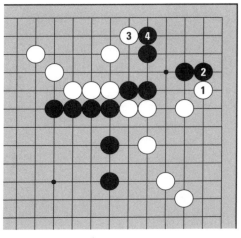

Answer 25

Diagram 4:

If White misses the chance to play these sente endgame moves, Black can seize the initiative with 1 and 3. White needs to respond at 2 and 4 to save the side territory.

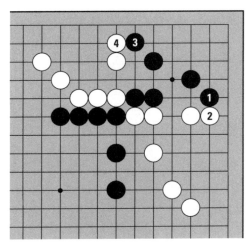

Diagram 4

Diagram 5:

Continuing from the previous diagram, White will lose even more ground since Black can play the hane-block-connect sequences from A to D in sente. Compared to *Answer 25*, this is a ten-point territory swing to Black's advantage.

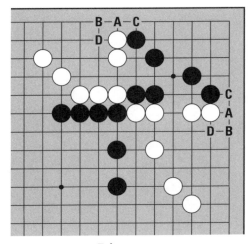

Diagram 5

SAMPLE OPENINGS

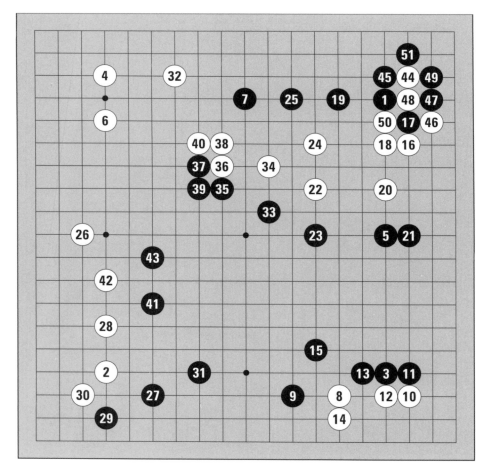

Game 1 (1 - 51)

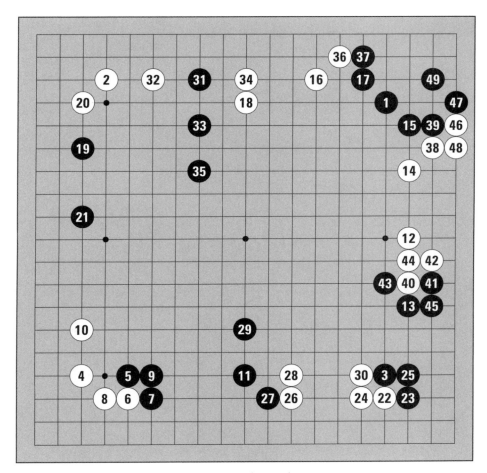

Game 2 (1 - 49)

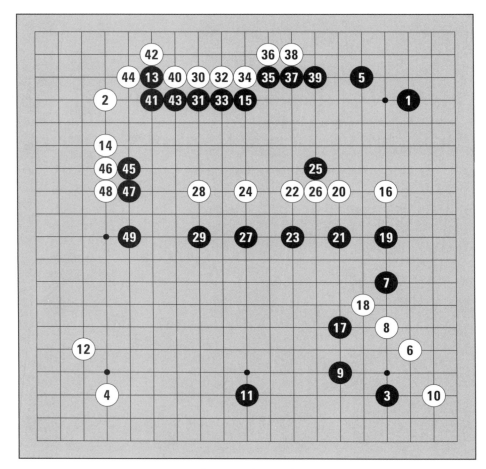

Game 3 (1 - 49)

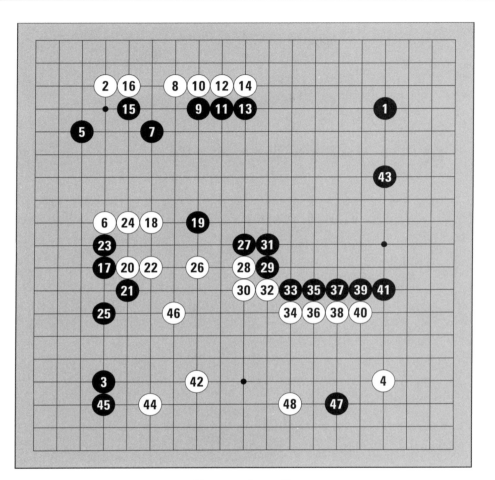

Game 4 (1 - 48)

Go on the Internet

Despite all the hype about the Internet, for go players the Net is truly a boon. It provides access to a vast array of information that might take years to track down through legwork and word of mouth, all at the click of a mouse. It also offers resources that are in some ways better than anything available in meat space (as the truly addicted are wont to call the off-line world).

As with all things Internet, the first step toward enjoying them is getting "Internet Access." (Well, the second step, actually. Naturally, first you need a computer.) If you don't already have Net access, look in local newspapers for ads by "internet service providers." You can usually get a connection (called a "PPP account") for about $25/month (as of this writing). There are also lots of books available in book stores now about how to get access to and get around the Net. For the purposes of this chapter, I'll assume you are connected and know how to get around (for example, that you can use a web browser like Netscape's Navigator).

Go Web Pages

There are many, many Web pages devoted to go, and like everything on the web, they range from the useful and entertaining (Go News from Japan, http://www.cwi.nl/~jansteen/go/) to the esoteric (Designing a Go Board for the Visually Impaired, http://www.math.rpi.edu/~vanpag/tactlgo.html) to the bizarre

(Round Go Board Diagram Generator, http://www.youdzone.com/go.html). Without looking too hard you can find information and pointers to just about anything relating to go that you might want to know. Our Good Move Press/Samarkand site and on-line catalog is at http://www.samarkand.net/. A couple of excellent starting points are Jansteen's site http://www.cwi.nl/~jansteen/go/ and Ken Warkentyne's site at http://nngs.cosmic.org/hmkw/index.html. If these sites don't have it, they point to it... or point to something that points to it...

Go Servers

Perhaps the best go resources on the internet are the go servers. Go servers are basically electronic go clubs. They allow players from all over the world to log on and play, watch, and talk about go. Go servers are particularly valuable for players who don't live in big cities and thus may not have access to a big pool of opponents - just by connecting to the Internet, you automatically have a pool of thousands of opponents of all strengths. (Go servers are also an extremely valuable tool for doctoral students trying to postpone the moment of graduation.) The biggest and most well-established go server is the Internet Go Server (IGS). At any given time there are generally between 100 and 400 players logged into the IGS, with strengths ranging from 30 kyu to professional 9 dan. You can find all the information you need about how to access IGS at their web site: http://igs.joyjoy.net/. A smaller (and, some would say, cozier) IGS-type server is the No Name Go Server (NNGS) with information at http://nngs.cosmic.org/.

Although it is possible to use a go server with only a text terminal, if you wish to keep your eyesight intact, avoid this at all costs! Much better is to use a "client," a program that runs on your computer and mediates communication between your computer and the go server. A client will give you a nice graphical go board and a point-and-click interface. Clients are available for a number of platforms including Win95 and Mac. All are either free or shareware of some kind, and available by FTP from the Go Archive in directory /Go/clients.

Another go server is available at Microsoft's Gaming Zone http://www.zone.com/. This is a lot smaller, slicker, and if you don't mind playing in the parlor of the evil empire, may be more convenient for a newcomer to the game.

The Go Archive

The Go Archive is a repository of information about go, computer go, and go on the Net. You can download records of professional games, go problems, go-playing programs, programs for recording, viewing, and commenting games, programs to let you play go over the Net, and much more. The Go Archive is an FTP site located at ftp://igs.nyui.net/Go/ or ftp://ftp.nuri.net/Go/.

The Go Newsgroup

There is a Usenet Newsgroup demoted to go, called rec.games.go. Discussions there range from the pros and cons of various rule systems, to comments on books, to news and game records of professional tournaments, to life and death problems and their solutions, to discussions of go etiquette and philosophy. There also tends to be a lot of talk about various issues surrounding go servers and IGS in particular. Remember, as with all newsgroups, before posting please read the Go FAQ (Frequently Asked Questions) file, which is posted periodically and can be retrieved by FTP from the Go Archive.

The Go Teaching Ladder

The Go Teaching Ladder is one of the most underutilized go resources of the Net. The ladder is a system by which anyone can email their game record to a stronger player, and within a week or so get it back with comments. The idea is that every participant will, in exchange for having their games commented by stronger players, make comments on the games of weaker players. This is a tremendous resource for the serious student who doesn't have easy access to instruction. It is particularly convenient in conjunction with go servers, which can automatically mail you records of your games.

The format used for recording and exchanging games in the Go Teaching Ladder is called Smart Go Format, or SGF. SGF is a format for recording games, variations, diagrams, and comments. Programs to let you create and view SGF files can be found in the Go Archive.

Information about the Go ladder is available at http://www.iicm.edu/GTL/.

The Computer Go Mailing List

The computer go mailing list is a forum that uses email for discussion about computer go. You can subscribe to the mailing list by sending email with SUBSCRIBE as the body of the message to computer-go-request@hsc.fr. To unsubscribe, send mail again to computer-go-request (not to the list itself). Once you are subscribed, messages sent to will automatically be copied to all the other members of the mailing list. An archive of the last few years of discussion can be found at the Go Archive.

On a final note, remember that the Net is growing and evolving at a phenomenal rate; by the time you read this, some of the information given here may be outdated, and certainly many more resources will have become available. Don't be afraid to explore!

David A. Mechner

David is a 6 dan amateur go player and doctoral fellow in Neuroscience at New York University. He represented the US at the World Youth Championship in Paris in 1988, and ten years later is postponing the moment of his graduation by playing go and encouraging others in his program to do the same.

INDEX

Note on names: Chinese, Japanese, and Korean names in this book are given family name first.